Collins gem

Gemstones

Cally Oldershaw

Collins

An Imprint of HarperCollinsPublishers

ISBN-10: 0-00-723301-9
ISBN-13: 978-0-00-723301-4

ISBN-10: 0-06-089062-2 (in the United States)
ISBN-13: 978-0-06-089062-9
FIRST U.S. EDITION Published 2006

Design and project management by Cambridge Publishing Management Limited, Cambridge, United Kingdom

Printed and bound by Amadeus, Italy

10 09 08 07 06
9 8 7 6 5 4 3 2 1

CONTENTS

KEY TO THE CRYSTAL SYSTEM

Although there is no such thing as an "amorphous crystal," we
have included it in this key for identification purposes.

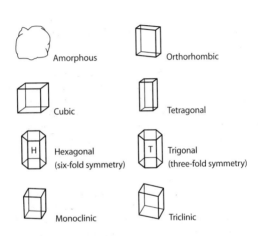

Amorphous

Orthorhombic

Cubic

Tetragonal

Hexagonal
(six-fold symmetry)

Trigonal
(three-fold symmetry)

Monoclinic

Triclinic

KEY TO THE HARDNESS SCALE

The relative hardness of each gemstone is indicated thus:
H3½ represents a gemstone with a hardness rating of 3½.

INTRODUCTION

This easy-to-use guide to gemstones contains more than 130 entries (145 pages) of full-color photographs with descriptions.

Divided into five sections, including a section on mineral gemstones and one on organic gemstones, this book guides you through the subject of gemology, and introduces you to the main gemstones used by jewelers, healers, and collected by gemstone enthusiasts. There is an entry for each gemstone, plus an extra introductory page for those with more than one gemstone in the "family"—for example, beryl, which includes emerald and aquamarine.

For each gemstone, there is a color photograph to help you recognize it. Photographs of well-cut gemstones show what they look like before they are set in jewelry. There are also photographs of gemstones set in spectacular pieces, designed to show them to their best advantage. The jewelry includes historical, famous, and modern pieces. Gemstones that are best polished, for example as slices for inlay or mosaic work, domed shapes (cabochons), cameos, intaglios, or carvings, are illustrated with appropriate photographs.

To help you find what you are looking for, each gemstone has information along the side of the page, which includes:

- a line diagram of the typical crystal shape
- the name of the gemstone
- the name of the gemstone "family"
- hardness
- the page number.

The text on each page tells you about each gemstone. You may want to know why the gemstone has the name that it has; for example, it may be because of its color, where it was found, or perhaps because of its chemistry.

Maybe you are interested in knowing a little of the history of the gemstone, who first found it, whether ancient civilizations held it in awe, and how they used it as a decorative gemstone, or perhaps even a weapon.

You might like to know about the myths and legends and the beliefs held by healers that are associated with some of the gemstones. Each gemstone has its own story to tell. This book is for you to find out some of those stories.

To help you use the book as a reference source, information is clearly shown in boxes and tables individually alongside each gemstone and at the back of the book. Turn to page 174 to find out more about what these headings mean:

- name
- chemical formula
- crystal system
- hardness
- Specific Gravity (SG)
- Refractive Index (RI)
- Birefringence (DR)
- luster.

HISTORY AND FASCINATION OF GEMSTONES

If you have ever walked along a beach and picked up a pebble, or seen something shining or twinkling on the ground and stopped to have a look, you will know the feeling of seeing that special something that catches your eye, that you want to have a better look at, that you may want to keep.

The outcome of this fascination is that gemstones have been coveted through the ages as something special, something even worth dying for. Surrounded by myths and legends, gemstones have attained a particular significance that has lasted for centuries; from prehistoric beads and ornaments to the present-day jewels of the royal families, engagement and wedding rings worn to celebrate marriage, and the "bling" worn by both men and women.

But what makes a gemstone? Gemstones have always been associated with adornment, wealth, and fame. Nowadays almost any material can be used to fashion jewelry for adornment for practically any part of the body, or to adorn fashion accessories such as shoes, handbags, and hats. Artists and sculptors may also use gemstones in their creations. Plastics, glass, wood, and clay are used in what is termed "costume jewelry," some are faceted and called "gems," but are they gemstones?

GEMSTONES: ATTRIBUTES

A gemstone is defined, by jewelers and gemologists (those who study gemstones scientifically), as having three attributes:

- beauty
- durability, and
- rarity.

Beauty

Beauty is essential for all gemstones, as the prime objective is to have an attractive product. But, as they say: "Beauty is in the eye of the beholder." A faceted gemstone may be preferred by some, while others find more beauty in an uncut rough crystal still in its "natural state."

Durability

Durability, the strength and hardness of a gemstone, determines how well it will last without becoming scratched, chipped, or worn. For a gemstone to keep its sparkle, not just for months or years, but for generations, it should be tough and have a hardness of more than 7 on the Mohs' scale (which measures the hardness of each gemstone on a scale of 1 to 10—see p176). It should also be treated with care. Softer materials can be cut as gemstones, but care must be taken in setting them in a way that protects them from wear and tear. Only diamond, with a hardness of 10, cannot be scratched by any other gemstone. Only a diamond can scratch a diamond, which is why this gemstone is considered the most long-lasting. Organic gemstones (see pp148–173) are generally not as hard as the mineral gemstones (see pp 26–147) and are fashioned accordingly.

Rarity

Rarity is a key attribute because, ultimately, it is the rarity that determines the value and it is the value that determines the market price of a gemstone. Rarity may refer to the rarity of the gem species, or the rarity of a particular gemstone—for example, because of a particularly rare color, a special locality, or unusual or record-breaking size.

FAMOUS GEMSTONES

The most famous gemstones are probably those that are the record breakers—for example, the largest, the oldest, or the first found. They may also be those with a fascinating or intriguing past—perhaps a story spanning many generations with tales of murder, or gemstones attributed with the properties of good or bad luck or a deathly curse. Additionally, they may be famous because of the people with whom they have become associated—for example, the Taylor-Burton Diamond.

A gem may have attained fame for several reasons—for example, the Hope Diamond is famous not only for its color (blue) but also its size, its history, and the history of its owners, who some believe have been cursed with bad luck as a consequence of owning the diamond.

There are tales of famous gemstones that have been re-cut or can no longer be traced; some are in private collections, others have been sold at auction to anonymous buyers, and yet others have simply disappeared. The whereabouts of many, though, is still known—for example, those in the palaces or vaults of royal families, national treasuries, or museum collections; and those owned by millionaires and celebrities.

Hope Diamond

Logan Sapphire

A diamond and sapphire necklace

MUSEUM COLLECTIONS

Below are just a few of the museums that have famous collections of gemstones and jewelry:

- USA: the Smithsonian Institution, and the American Museum of Natural History
- London, UK: the Tower of London, British Museum, Victoria and Albert Museum, and Natural History Museum
- Paris, France: the Louvre
- Germany: the gemstone museums of Idar-Oberstein and Green Vault, Dresden
- Istanbul, Turkey: the Topkapi Palace Museum
- St Petersburg, Russia: the State Hermitage Museum.

DIAMONDS: THE 4 CS

Rough diamonds are sorted (graded) depending on their crystal shape, size, and clarity before being sold to be cut and fashioned. In assessing the value of a cut diamond when buying or selling, those in the jewelry trade will take four attributes into account. These are generally referred to as the 4 Cs:

- color
- cut
- carat, and
- clarity.

Color

You may have heard a so-called "perfect" diamond being referred to as a "D flawless." This is the terminology used to describe a diamond with a color "D" (the whitest and cleanest color) and totally clear, without any flaws or imperfections. Most diamonds, however, have a slight hint or tinge of color, usually yellow or brown. Without training and practice, the very slight differences in colorless diamonds are difficult to see. It is not until about grade M that the yellow tinge becomes more obvious. The bright colored diamonds (including pink, yellow, blue, and green) are called fancy colored diamonds. They are described using different color schemes.

The GIA (Gemological Institute of America) color grading scheme (*see the table opposite*) is one of those that is used by professional jewelers.

Color grading	Description
D	Colorless
E	
F	
G	Nearly Colorless
H	
I	
J	
K	Faintly Yellow
L	
M	
N	Very Light Yellow
O	
P	
Q	
R	
S	Light Yellow
T	
U	
V	
W	
X	
Y	
Z	
Z+	Fancy colored diamonds

Cut

The shape of the cut and the make of the cut (how exactly it has been cut) are taken into account when assessing the cut of a diamond. The round brilliant cut is the most popular cut for a diamond. The angles and dimensions of an "ideal brilliant" are worked out mathematically (for example, by diamond cutter Marcel Tolkowsky in 1919) to give the best possible shape and number of flat polished faces (facets) to ensure that light which enters the gemstone is reflected back towards the eye of the viewer. A well-cut brilliant diamond will sparkle, showing flashes of all the colors of the rainbow ("fire"); a badly-cut one will appear dull and lack "fire."

Other traditional shapes used include the step cut, rose cut, cushion cut, baguette, marquise, rectangular, and square cut.

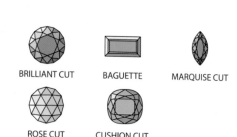

BRILLIANT CUT   BAGUETTE   MARQUISE CUT

ROSE CUT   CUSHION CUT

Examples of some traditional shapes for cutting diamonds

With the introduction of computer technology and the use of lasers in gemstone cutting, modern cuts are far more varied, including fancy shapes such as kite, heart, cross, and hexagon.

Carat

The unit of weight used to measure diamonds is the carat (0.2g) (g = gram). The name is thought to have been derived from the carob, which is now used as a chocolate substitute. Each seed or bean of the carob is nearly identical in weight. Traditionally, a one carat diamond was the same as the weight of one carob bean, though it is now standardized as 0.2g. In the Far East, rice was used as a comparison and one carob bean equaled four grains of rice. There are 100 points in a carat, so half a carat diamond will weigh 50 points.

Clarity

The clarity grading of a diamond is an assessment of its inclusions and flaws. Internal flaws ("inclusions" are one type of "flaw") include, for example, cracks, air bubbles, and the presence of other minerals within the diamond. Surface features include scratches, chipped areas, and pits, which are also assessed. Surface flaws (also called blemishes) may be caused as a result of cutting and polishing, and care should be taken to check the girdle (the widest part of the stone), which separates the crown (top) from the pavilion (bottom) of the gemstone for marks. The cleaner the diamond, the better its clarity grade, and the more valuable it is.

Grading (*see the table opposite*) is carried out using a strong light and a ×10 magnifying lens. The grade, and therefore the value and price, are affected by the inclusions, but as no difference can be seen between a flawless diamond (categorized as F) and one with slight inclusions (categorized as SI) without the ×10 magnification, they look the same to the naked eye. It is only when the clarity reaches the grade I1 (imperfect 1) that the flaws can be seen.

Gem-testing laboratories can prepare a "plot" (line drawing or sketch) of a diamond's inclusions, and include this on a diamond-grading certificate. In the same way that no two people will have the same fingerprint, no two diamonds will have the same clarity plot.

Clarity Grading	Description
F	Flawless. No internal or external flaws. Extremely rare.
IF	Internally Flawless. No internal flaws, but some surface flaws. Very rare.
VVS1–VVS2	Very Very Slightly Included (two grades, VVS1 is the least included). Minute inclusions very difficult to detect under ×10 magnification by a trained gemologist.
VS1–VS2	Very Slightly Included (two grades). Minute inclusions seen only with difficulty under ×10 magnification by a trained gemologist.
SI1–SI2	Slightly Included (two grades). Minute inclusions more easily detected under ×10 magnification.
I1–I2–I3	Included (three grades). Inclusions visible under ×10 magnification. Inclusions also visible to the naked eye.

CAT'S-EYES AND STAR STONES

Some gemstones have oriented inclusions that reflect light in such a way that when they are cut *en cabochon* (as a rounded polished dome), they show a bright line or star across the surface of the gemstone. Parallel elongate, needle-like, or fibrous inclusions will result in a line, also known as a cat's-eye—because of the similarity to the eye of a cat. Gemstones showing a cat's-eye may be called chatoyant after the French word *chat* ("cat"). When inclusions intersect, they may produce a star stone (the effect is called asterism). Star stones may have four, six, or sometimes twelve "arms" to the star.

Rosser Reeves Star Ruby

Star of Asia (sapphire)

SYNTHETIC AND SIMULATED GEMSTONES

The value and appeal of gemstones are such that those who cannot acquire the "real thing" will consider the option of having something that has the appearance of the gemstone that they desire. There are records of turquoise imitations in Egyptian tombs, glass imitations of gems have been found in Roman ruins, and no doubt this practice goes back much further. With modern technologies, gemstones can now be made in the laboratory.

Synthetic gemstones

Synthetic gemstones have the same chemical composition as the natural equivalent gemstone. Because of this, they also have the same optical and physical properties—that is, they look the same. Corundum (sapphires and rubies) has been made synthetically in the laboratory since 1902. The Frenchman, Auguste Verneuil, developed the Verneuil process, melting the chemical ingredients then allowing them to cool and form a candle-shaped piece of synthetic ruby ("boule"), which could be faceted to imitate natural ruby. Most gemstones can be produced synthetically in the laboratory; these include: diamond, emerald, chrysoberyl, spinel, quartz, and many more. Synthetic chatoyant (cat's-eye stones) and star stones can be produced by introducing the element titanium into the process.

Simulated gemstones

Imitation gemstones can be made of any material. They do not have the same chemistry as the natural equivalent. Paste (man-made glass) has been used to imitate many gemstones. Victorian paste was colored to imitate emerald, ruby, and sapphire. A gemstone of a lesser value can also be used to imitate a more valuable gemstone, for example howlite (a white, chalky mineral) has been stained to imitate turquoise, and red garnet has been used to imitate ruby.

Man-made gemstones that have no natural equivalent, for example CZ (cubic zirconia), are called artificial gemstones or artificial man-made gemstones; they are not synthetic gemstones. CZ can be made in many different colors, and has been used to imitate diamond, ruby, sapphire, emerald, and other gemstones.

Above right: Koh-i-Noor replica
Below right: Imitation emerald

GEMSTONE TREATMENTS

The majority of gems on the market are routinely enhanced or treated in some way. Some treatments are so common, such as the oiling of emeralds and the heat treatment of sapphires, that they are seldom disclosed. However, disclosure of all treatments should be encouraged, and all jewelers should be aware of what they are selling. In the jewelry business, the most important asset is reputation. Reputations built up, sometimes over several generations, can be lost in an instant by not disclosing certain treatments. A gemstone should only be referred to as natural and untreated if it is just that.

Surface treatments

These treatments include waxing, oiling, enameling, inking, foiling, or covering the surface with a thin film. The treatments are carried out in order to enhance the color of the gemstone, improve its appearance by hiding cracks or flaws, or increase its value by adding special effects (such as iridescence). Surface treatments are not permanent: oils may be lost due to drying out, and enameling, inking, and so on can be rubbed off or scratched. Therefore, extra care should be taken when handling or wearing gemstones with this type of treatment.

Shallow treatments

Diffusion treatments involve heating and introducing chemicals which affect the surface and a thin layer below the surface of a gemstone. These treatments may enhance the color or seal porous gemstones to protect them against drying out. They may also be used to produce cat's-eye and star stones. This type of treatment is usually permanent.

Heat treatment and irradiation

Much of the ruby, sapphire, and aquamarine on the market is routinely heat treated. Heat treatment is permanent and an acceptable practice. It is used to enhance or change color, or to improve clarity. Other gemstones that may be heat treated include: amethyst (changing its color to the more valuable citrine) and tanzanite (to remove brown coloration and improve the vibrant blue of the gemstone).

Heat treatment may be used in conjunction with irradiation. Gemstones are irradiated with electron or gamma irradiation to improve their color and clarity. The treatment is considered permanent and, although it may occasionally fade with time, it is unlikely that any difference will be noticeable over the lifetime of the owner. Examples include: the irradiation and heating of pale or colorless topaz to give the vibrant blues popular in jewelry; heating quartz to produce citrine, amethyst, and ametrine (a gemstone comprising both amethyst and citrine); and pale pink tourmaline to the neon pink or hot pink tourmaline.

"MINERAL" GEMSTONES

The gemstones in this part are all minerals. Minerals are naturally occurring materials that are the building blocks of earth's rocks. Each mineral has a unique chemical composition (chemical formula). Minerals are sorted into groups or families of gemstones depending on their chemistry and their color.

The gemstones here are mainly those that can be cut as faceted gemstones, with many flat, polished surfaces—for example, diamond, ruby, and sapphire. They are generally transparent, hard-wearing, and have warm or bright colors, making them attractive gemstones for use in jewelry. However, there are some gemstones—for example, azurite, fluorite, malachite, and rhodochrosite—that are fairly soft and can easily be scratched.

AZURITE

Azurite

In the Middle Ages, azurite was popular as a dye and a pigment used in paints. Its name is derived from the Persian word *lajvard* ("blue"). The wonderfully rich, dark blue of azurite is shown at its best in azurmalachite, alongside bands of the bright green mineral malachite. Carved or polished pieces may be waxed. This is to protect what is a fairly soft mineral from scratching.

Occurrence Mainly in copper-mining areas such as Africa, Australia, Chile, China, and Russia. Azurite found in Chessy (France) is called chessylite.

CAMEO/CARVED

BERYL
Beryl

Beryl is the name given to a group of gems which share a similar chemical composition (beryllium aluminum silicate). Beryl is colorless, but small amounts of impurities, elements called trace elements, color the gemstones. The best known is the green emerald. Others are aquamarine (blue-green), heliodor (yellow), morganite (pink), goshenite (colorless), and the rare bixbite (red beryl).

Occurrence Beryl is found worldwide. The largest gemstones are found in igneous rocks called pegmatites. World-record gems have been found in the pegmatites of Brazil. The best emerald is found in Colombia.

AQUAMARINE
Beryl

H7½

Named after the Latin *aqua* (water) and *mare* (marine or sea), the clear-blue seawater color of aquamarine is a popular gemstone. Often free from inclusions and found as large crystals or pebbles, it is fairly easy to

cut and a favorite with gemstone designers and engravers. Most aquamarine is heat-treated to improve its color and remove tinges of yellow or brown caused by iron. The color change is permanent and is an acceptable practice by those in the jewelry trade. Pale blue aquamarine can also be irradiated to darken its color. These dark blue irradiated stones are called blue beryl. Aquamarine is the birthstone for March.

Occurrence Much of the aquamarine used in jewelry is from Brazil, particularly from Minas Gerais, an area in the southeast of the country. Aquamarines are also found in other countries, including Afghanistan, Madagascar, Mozambique, Nigeria, Pakistan, and Zambia.

CABOCHON   FACETED

Emerald

H7½

EMERALD
Beryl

The best known of the beryl group, the vivid green emerald color is caused by the trace elements chromium and vanadium. The name derives from the word *smargus*, which means "green gemstone" in Ancient Greek. Emeralds are

seldom clear, but contain a miniature world of inclusions. Characteristic inclusions of certain minerals or patterns can be used to find out not just the country from which the emerald came, but also the mine. Emeralds are usually oiled with polymers and epoxies to fill cracks and inclusions and enhance the color and appearance of the stone. They should be re-oiled every few years, and should not be cleaned using ultrasonic cleaners. Emerald is the birth-stone for May.

Occurrence The Colombian mines of Chivor and Muzo are famous for their emeralds. The Coscuez mines are the largest source of Colombian emeralds, with as much as 50 percent of all emeralds coming from Colombia. Other sources include Afghanistan, Bahaia in Brazil, the Copperbelt of northern Zambia, and North Carolina (USA).

CABOCHON   FACETED

GOSHENITE

Beryl

Goshenite is colorless because it doesn't have sufficient trace elements (impurities) to color it. Named after Goshen, Hampshire County, Massachusetts, where it was first found, goshenite is also known as white beryl or lucid beryl. The Ancient Greeks fashioned spectacle lenses from goshenite. More recently it has been used to imitate other gemstones—for example, diamond by placing silver foil behind the stone in a piece of jewelry, or emerald by using colored foil. Goshenite, like the other beryls, can be irradiated to change its color to blue or yellow.

Occurrence Localities include Brazil, Canada, China, Pakistan, Russia, and the USA.

CABOCHON

FACETED

HELIODOR
Beryl

H7½

Named after its pale yellow or golden-yellow color, from the Greek *helios* and *doros*, meaning "gift from the sun." Heliodor was discovered in Namibia in 1910. The color is due to traces of iron, which may also cause the stone to have a greenish yellow or brown color. The pale yellow heliodor from Brazil is often step cut to give it a stronger color. Beryl can be irradiated to give dark golden stones, called golden beryl or heliodorite.

Occurrence The best-quality stones are found in the Urals of Russia. Other localities include Brazil, Madagascar, Namibia, Nigeria, Ukraine, and the USA.

FACETED

MORGANITE
Beryl

H7½

Colored by manganese, the bright lilac-pink beryl, morganite, was discovered in Madagascar in 1891 and named after J Pierpont Morgan (an American banker with an interest in gemstones) by George Kunz (after whom another pink gemstone, kunzite, is named). Morganite can be heat-treated to remove traces of yellow or orange caused by iron to give a more attractive and purer pink stone. Morganite is pleochroic, looking colorless when viewed from one direction, and pink from another. For this reason, it is important to set the stone correctly so that the best color is seen through the front of the stone.

Occurrence Brazil, Madagascar, Namibia, Pakistan, Southern California, and Zimbabwe.

FACETED

RED BERYL (BIXBITE)
Beryl

Red beryl is the rarest of the beryl group, and is seldom seen as a cut stone because most crystals are too small to facet as gemstones. It has only been found in three places, all in the USA. Originally named after Maynard Bixby, who discovered the gemstone in 1904 in the Thomas Mountains in Utah, it has since been found in the Wah Wah Mountains, also in Utah, and the Black Mountains of southwest New Mexico. It occurs in volcanic rocks called rhyolites. The red color is caused by manganese.

Occurrence New Mexico and Utah.

FACETED

MICROCRYSTALLINE QUARTZ (CHERT AND CHALCEDONY)

Microcrystalline quartz

Quartz may occur as transparent crystals such as the colorless rock crystal, purple amethyst, or yellow-golden citrine (macrocrystalline), or may have crystals so small they can only be seen with the aid of a microscope (microcrystalline). Gemologists tend to refer to all microcrystalline quartz that can be fashioned as gemstones as chalcedony. However, not all microcrystalline quartz is chalcedony. There are, in fact, two varieties of microcrystalline quartz: chalcedony and chert. Chalcedony has a fibrous texture comprised of microscopic elongated "fibrous" quartz crystals e.g. agate. Chert is comprised of more "granular" microscopic quartz crystals e.g. chert, flint and jasper. Bloodstone may be either fibrous or granular. Named after Chalcedon (also known as Calchedon), an ancient port near present-day Istanbul in Turkey, chalcedony is divided, somewhat arbitrarily, into those specimens that are predominantly a solid color or have straight bands, and those that have curved lines or bands (agate). Different-colored chalcedony has different names—for example, the reddish-brown carnelian, apple-green chrysoprase or heliotrope with red spots.

H7

Occurrence Microcrystalline quartz is found worldwide.

BANDED AGATE

Microcrystalline quartz

Agate occurs in hard nodular rocks, or geodes, which, when broken open, reveal chalcedony with intricate patterns of concentric banding in a wide range of colors. The nodules are found in igneous rocks and lavas. There may be a hole or a block of a single color towards the center of the pattern, and a small pipe or exit route marked towards the edge. Agate may have curved lines or bands interspersed with bands of crystals that may be colorless quartz or colored by impurities. Romans Pliny the Elder and the poet Silius Italicus quote in their writings that agate had been found for the first time in Sicily, in the Achates River, from which the stone took the name. Agates are given descriptive names after their appearance—for example, Cyclops agate (from Mexico), star agate, and cloud agate. They may be transparent, translucent (allow light through), or opaque. Thin slices of translucent agate may be used as decorative panels in lampshades, or as wall hangings or light catchers.

Occurrence Agate is found worldwide. The most famous historical locality is the Idar-Oberstein region of Germany, where agate has been collected since Roman times. There are records of mining in the region since 1548, and it remains a gem-trading center, but most agate is now imported from Brazil and Uruguay.

CABOCHON

CAMEO/CARVED

POLISHED

STAINED/DYED AGATE
Microcrystalline quartz

H7

Agate may be dyed or stained to give a wide range of colors. Dyes and stains may be used to brighten the grays, browns, oranges, and greens. They may also be used to color agate bright colors that are not found in natural agates, such as the ink blue, neon blue, and neon pink agate that can be seen sliced and fashioned as book ends or decorative wall or window hangings. Blue-stained agates are called Swiss lapis or false lapis after the blue lapis lazuli.

Agates have probably been stained since Roman times and maybe even before. The usual method is the sugar-acid treatment (*see* **onyx**, *p46*), though the range of modern synthetic dyes and stains allows for the use of modern techniques.

Occurrence Dyed/stained agates can now be found in shops and markets worldwide.

CABOCHON

CAMEO/CARVED

POLISHED

MOSS "AGATE"/MOCHA STONE
Microcrystalline quartz

Moss agate has a milky white, grayish to bluish white, or colorless background (matrix) with mineral impurities or inclusions such as chlorite that forms greenish branch-like dendritic patterns or other plant-like patterns such as mosses, leaves, and trees. Moss agate, also known as mocha stone, has black, brown, or dark green mineral inclusions that resemble moss. Manganese oxides are a common inclusion in moss agate, as are iron oxides and iron hydroxides. Where inclusions resemble trees and other features of a land-scape the specimen may be called landscape agate.

Occurrence Localities include Brazil, China, India, Scotland, and the USA.

CABOCHON

CAMEO/CARVED

POLISHED

H7

FORTIFICATION AGATE

Microcrystalline quartz

Fortification agate has patterns of angular lines and bands that resemble the outline of a fortress as seen from the air. Bands are generally pale grays and browns with white, though brighter colors may also be found. Margins may be crenulated (with square outlines) or have a zigzag angular outline. Ruin agate describes agate that resembles the profile outline of a town or village.

Occurrence Localities include Brazil, China, India, Madagascar, Mexico, Scotland, South Africa, and the USA.

CABOCHON

CAMEO/CARVED

POLISHED

LANDSCAPE AGATE
Microcrystalline quartz

H7

Although strictly a jasper rather than an agate, as it doesn't usually show banding, this stone is referred to as landscape agate. Dark mineral inclusions such as iron oxides and iron hydroxides can form intricate tree and branch-like dendritic patterns, which may resemble landscapes with hills and trees. Lakes, islands, and other landscape features may also be found in landscape agates. Landscape agate may be fashioned as polished or sliced pieces, mounted in picture frames or small lockets, or as carved pieces for brooches or necklaces.

Occurrence Localities include China, Brazil, Germany, India, Madagascar, Mexico, Scotland, South Africa, and the USA.

CABOCHON

CAMEO/CARVED

POLISHED

FIRE AGATE
Microcrystalline quartz

The iridescent colors of
fire agate are similar to
the play of color of opals.
In fire agates, the patchy
iridescent colors are caused
by the reflection of light off
layers of iron oxide minerals
(goethite) within the quartz. The rainbow effect or "fire" may be
enhanced by cutting the piece *en cabochon* (with a rounded
top), or by polishing as a rounded bead or irregular piece with
a rounded surface. Fire agate, with its oily iridescence, has only
been commercially available since the 1950s when trading of
rough pieces from Mexico was established. The red color is
most sought-after, while the less attractive browns and yellows
are less valuable.

Occurrence Agate is found worldwide. Main localities for
fire agate are Mexico and the USA, particularly Arizona.

CABOCHON

CAMEO/CARVED

POLISHED

IRIS AGATE/RAINBOW AGATE
Microcrystalline quartz

Iris agate is iridescent. Light is diffracted; it is split into the spectral colors. The spectral colors are the colors of the rainbow, which is why iris agate may also be called rainbow agate. The diffraction is a result of light being reflected from many thin parallel layers, called lamellae, which are within the quartz (chalcedony) of the gemstone. The lamellae are made up of light

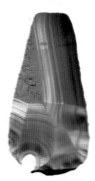

and dark bands of microcrystalline quartz with different properties. The light bands are made up of larger micro-crystalline crystals of quartz that spiral one way (either right or left). The darker bands are made up of smaller micro-crystalline crystals that have an alternating pattern of left and right spirals. The pattern repeats itself thousands of times in these agates.

Occurrence Agate is found worldwide.

CABOCHON

CAMEO/CARVED

POLISHED

H7

BLUE LACE AGATE
Microcrystalline quartz

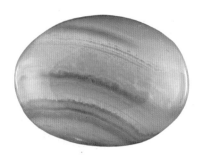

The delicate lace-like patterns of blue lace agate make an attractive gemstone when polished or carved. The delicacy of the pattern and the blue color are thought by some to instill a feeling of calm and peace, and are used to help with meditation and spiritual connection. Polished blue lace agate has been used as gemstones in brooches, pendants, necklaces, and bracelets.

Occurrence Agate is found worldwide.

CABOCHON

CAMEO/CARVED

POLISHED

BULL'S-EYE AGATE/ CYCLOPS AGATE

Microcrystalline quartz

H7

Where the agate is cut and polished to show a single "eye" it may be called Bull's-eye agate or Cyclops agate, after the one-eyed monster of Greek mythology. Cyclops agate, with the single "eye" formed from concentric layers of red and white chalcedony, was found in Chihuahua, Mexico, in about 1895 by Mr. E. J. Smith, who proposed the name.

Occurrence Agate with a single "eye" is found in a number of localities, including Mexico.

CABOCHON

CAMEO/CARVED

POLISHED

ONYX
Microcrystalline quartz

Onyx is a granular microcrystalline quartz and should strictly be termed chert rather than chalcedony. Onyx has straight stripes of alternating black and white or brown and white.

Found mainly in Mexico, natural black onyx is rare, and much of the black onyx on the market is stained or dyed chert or chalcedony. Records show that agates have been stained by the ancient Romans and ancient Egyptians. The usual method is the sugar-acid treatment. Agate is dipped in a sugar solution which penetrates the porous rock, following cracks and flaws within the piece and the lines of the banding. The agate is then heated in sulfuric acid, which carbonizes the sugar, darkening it and turning it black.

Occurrence Localities include Afghanistan, Brazil, India, Madagascar, Mexico, Peru, and the USA.

CABOCHON

CAMEO/CARVED

POLISHED

SARD
Microcrystalline quartz

Sard is a granular microcrystalline quartz and should strictly be termed chert rather than chalcedony. Sard is red-brown in color and generally not as bright as carnelian (also known as cornelian) and with more of a brown tint. Sard may be imitated by soaking chalcedony with an iron solution that has the effect of staining it to give it the rust color of sard, in much the same way as iron will rust. Named after the Greek word *sardios* and Latin *sarda*, the town of Sardis, the ancient capital of Lydia (now Turkey) where the stone was found.

Occurrence Localities include China, India, Sri Lanka, and the USA.

CABOCHON

CAMEO/CARVED

POLISHED

H7

SARDONYX
Microcrystalline quartz

Sardonyx combines the black of onyx and the red-brown of sard with the white stripes of both. Sardonyx may contain both chert and chalcedony microcrystalline quartz. Because of their layered or striped structure, sard, onyx, and sardonyx are particularly well suited to being carved as cameos or intaglios. In a cameo, the image (for example, a flower) or outline of a portrait remains, while the layers that make up the background are removed. An intaglio is the opposite, with the image incised—for example, for use as a wax seal. Onyx seals were popular with the Romans.

Occurrence The Sardonyx Mountains of India remain a major source. Other localities include Australia, Brazil, China, Madagascar, Sri Lanka, the Ural Mountains of Russia, Uruguay, and the USA.

CABOCHON

CAMEO/CARVED

POLISHED

CHRYSOPRASE/PRASE
Microcrystalline quartz

The translucent apple-green chalcedony popular with both the Greeks and the Romans is still the most valued chalcedony. The color is due to the presence of nickel. The even color and texture of chrysoprase makes it ideal for use as beads and cameos. Agate has been stained to imitate chrysoprase, while the best-quality chrysoprase may look similar to jade and has been

H7

marketed as Imperial jade or Australian jade. Prase is a less bright, but far rarer, leek-green chalcedony, found in Eastern Europe and the USA. Plasma is another name given to green chalcedony, but it lacks the bright apple-green of chrysoprase.

Occurrence Historically, the finest material was mined in Poland and the Czech Republic. Since the discovery of fine chrysoprase in Queensland in 1965, Australia has become a main source. Other localities include Germany, Russia, and the USA.

CAMEO/CARVED   POLISHED

Jasper

H7

JASPER
Microcrystalline quartz

Jasper is the red, brown, or yellow opaque massive microcrystalline quartz. Strictly a chert, colored by iron oxides, green chlorite, or actinolite, it may show a combination of colors in patches or stripes. Orbicular jasper has a "gobstopper" (hard spherical sweet with concentric layers) or eyeball pattern with white or gray. Riband jasper is striped. Gray-colored hornstone resembles the horn of a cow or ox. Ancient Egyptians, Greeks, and Romans fashioned jasper as cameo and intaglio portraits, and also as beads or pieces for brooches, earrings, and necklaces. Fossil wood replaced by jasper shows the growth rings, for example in the fossil forests of Arizona, USA.

Occurrence Jasper occurs worldwide, though some areas are best known for particular types of jasper—for example, the riband jasper of the Urals of Russia; red and green jasper of Kazakhstan; and the red jasper of India and Venezuela. Other localities include Chile, Egypt, Libya, the UK, and the USA.

CAMEO/CARVED   POLISHED

CARNELIAN/CORNELIAN
Microcrystalline quartz

H7

The orange and reddish translucent microcrystalline quartz, carnelian (also called cornelian), has been used since ancient times polished as beads or *en cabochon*, or fashioned as cameos or intaglios. It may be uniformly colored or show faint banding. The major sources of carnelian are India, Brazil, Uruguay, and Japan, but much of the carnelian on the market is heat-treated to improve its color, enhancing the red and removing the brown. Carnelian has been used to "still the blood" and calm the temper.

Occurrence Major sources are Brazil, India, Japan, and Uruguay. Other localities include Australia, England, France, Germany, Madagascar, Russia, and the USA.

CABOCHON

CAMEO/CARVED

POLISHED

BLOODSTONE/ HELIOTROPE/ PLASMA

Microcrystalline quartz

Bloodstone is the green opaque microcrystalline quartz with red spots (due to iron oxides) that resemble blood, hence its name.

H7

It is also known as heliotrope. Plasma is another spotted microcrystalline quartz; it is green and opaque, but the spots are yellow or yellow-brown rather than red. Because of the blood-red spots of bloodstone, it has long been associated with blood, making athletes stronger and also stopping bleeding. In medieval times, it gained religious conn-otations as spots were said to signify the red splashes of Christ's blood, spilled when he was on the Cross. Healing powers were then attributed to the stone, and it was worn as a talisman. In Germany, bloodstone is the name given to the mineral hematite, so the chalcedony is sometimes called bluestone to avoid confusion.

Occurrence India is the main locality. Other localities include Australia, Brazil, China, and the USA.

CABOCHON

CAMEO/CARVED

POLISHED

CHRYSOBERYL
Chrysoberyl

H8½

Chrysoberyl occurs in a range of colors with a range of chemical compositions. Most chrysoberyl is yellow, yellowish-green, green, greenish-brown, or brown. The relative hardness and high refractive index make chryso-beryl an attractive gemstone. Where the gemstone shows a cat's-eye effect when cut *en cabochon* (as a cabochon) it is referred to as cat's-eye or cymophane. Alexandrite is the best-known variety of chrysoberyl, with its wonderful color change from green in daylight to red in incandescent light (for example, the artificial light of a light bulb); it is also the most valuable. The name chrysoberyl is de-rived from the Greek *chrysos*, meaning "golden," and *beryllos*, because it contains the chemical element, beryllium.

Occurrence Historically, the best chrysoberyl locality was in the Urals of Russia. Other localities include Brazil, China, Myanmar, Sri Lanka, Tanzania, and Zimbabwe.

CABOCHON   FACETED

ALEXANDRITE
Chrysoberyl

Alexandrite is the famous color-change variety of chrysoberyl. The best alexandrite shows green under fluorescent lights and red under incandescent light. Said to have been found in 1830 on the birthday of Tsar Alexander II and named in his honor by the mineralogist, Nils Nordenskjold. The color change is due to chromium, which partly replaces aluminum in the chemical composition of the gemstone.

Occurrence The finest alexandrite was found in the Urals of Russia. More recently, discoveries in Brazil (1987), India, Mozambique (1993), and Tanzania have produced fine gemstones.

FACETED

CHRYSOLITE (PALE YELLOW)
Chrysoberyl

H8½

Chrysolite, historically, is a name that has been used to describe pale yellow chrysoberyl which was popular in 18th and 19th century Portuguese jewelry and should not be confused with the pale-yellow green peridot (olivine) of the same name (see page 109). Found in granites, pegmatites, and schists, or recovered from alluvial sands and gravels, the hard-wearing gemstones are harder than most gemstones—only ruby, sapphire, and diamond are harder. Crystals may be found twinned, the change in the growth of a gem's crystal direction. A particular twin associated with chrysoberyl is a triple twin or "trilling," which gives the twinned crystals a hexagonal (six-sided) outline.

Occurrence Chrysolite, as with darker yellows, green, and brown chrysoberyl, occurs in localities including Brazil, India, Mozambique, Myanmar, Russia, Sri Lanka, the USA, and Zimbabwe.

CABOCHON

FACETED

CYMOPHANE
Chrysoberyl

Where chrysoberyl is cut *en cabochon* (cut as a cabochon) and shows a cat's-eye effect (also known as chatoyancy) it may be called cymophane or cat's-eye. Only a chrysoberyl cat's-eye may be referred to as cat's-eye; all other gemstones that show a cat's-eye should be referred to using their name—for example, a sapphire cat's-eye (or chatoyant sapphire), a quartz cat's-eye (or chatoyant quartz), etc. The cat's-eye effect is caused by light reflecting off parallel-oriented groups of inclusions within the gemstone, which gives a thin bright line across the surface of the stone, similar to that of a cat's-eye.

Occurrence Localities include Brazil, India, Mozambique, Myanmar, Russia, Sri Lanka, the USA, and Zimbabwe.

CABOCHON

FACETED

CORUNDUM
Corundum

Corundum is famous
for its rubies and
sapphires. With a
hardness of 9 on Mohs'
scale, only diamond
is harder (10). The
chemical composition
of corundum is very
simple, only aluminum
and oxygen, and all

corundum would be colorless if it did not contain small
amounts of other elements—for example, ruby is colored by
the presence of chromium, and blue sapphire by iron and
titanium. Ruby (red) and padparadscha (pinkish-orange) are
the only members of the corundum family that have separate
names; all the others are referred to as "fancy sapphires"—for
example, green sapphire and pink sapphire. If a gemstone is
simply referred to as a sapphire, it is assumed it is blue.
Sapphire is one of the birthstones for September.

Occurrence Found in metamorphic rocks and in gem
gravels. Localities include Afghanistan, Australia, Cambodia,
China, Greece, India, Japan, Madagascar, Myanmar, Nigeria,
Russia, Scotland, Sri Lanka, Thailand, and the USA.

COLORLESS SAPPHIRE

Corundum

Pure sapphire is colorless. Colorless sapphires are quite common, but most are heated to give colored gemstones. Also, because of their relatively simple chemistry, sapphire and ruby have been made synthetically in the laboratory for more than a hundred years (1902). The different colors can be made by adding the appropriate trace elements.

Until the end of the 19th century sapphires were often given names of gems that they were similar to, with the prefix "oriental." Green sapphire could be referred to as oriental emerald or oriental peridot depending on the color. Because of the confusion this caused, it is now common practice to call all corundum (except the red, ruby) sapphire, with their color as the prefix—for example, green sapphire. Sapphires that are not blue are often referred to as fancy sapphires. Green sapphire is, therefore, a fancy sapphire. The green may range from a pale green, through yellowish-green and bluish-green to dark emerald-green.

In the Verneuil process, the powdered ingredients are heated so that they melt. The melt drips onto a revolving plate. As it cools it solidifies with the same chemical composition and optical properties as natural corundum. There are several methods of producing synthetic gemstones. The Verneuil method produces a candle-like shape, called a boule. It can then be cut and polished as gemstones. Other methods may produce synthetic gems with crystal shapes. Colorless sapphire has been known as oriental white sapphire.

Occurrence Localities include Australia, Cambodia, China, Greece, India, Japan, Madagascar, Myanmar, Russia, Scotland, Sri Lanka, Thailand, and the USA. Green sapphires can be found in Africa (Tanzania), Queensland and New South Wales (Australia), Sri Lanka, and Thailand.

FACETED

PADPARADSCHA
Corundum

H9

Named after the Sin-
halese phrase *padma
radschen* signifying the
color of the lotus flower
or lotus blossom,
padparadscha is a
rare yellowish-pink or
orange-pink colored
sapphire. The color is
caused by very small
amounts of the chemical
elements chromium and
iron. Orange and yellow
sapphires may be heat-treated
or irradiated to intensify their color.

Occurrence Sri Lanka is the main locality for fancy
sapphires, including padparadscha. They have also been found
in Madagascar and Vietnam. Gem-quality orange and orange-
brown sapphire is found in the Umba Valley in northeast
Tanzania. Although it usually lacks the pink color
tinge, it is sometimes called African padparadscha.

FACETED

PINK SAPPHIRE
Corundum

H9

Pink sapphires that lack the chromium needed to give the red ruby color still make a very attractive and hard-wearing gemstone. Although the correct name is pink sapphire, pale pinkish-purple sapphire has sometimes been known as "oriental amethyst," and a darker pink or purple sapphire called Bengal amethyst. To avoid confusion neither of the two names should be used. Pink sapphires are thought to protect the wearer from misfortune if worn on the skin. For this reason, sapphires may be cut and fashioned so that the back of the gemstone touches the skin. A deeper cut and thicker stone will also serve to intensify the color of a pale gemstone.

Occurrence Most sapphires are from Australia, Brazil, Madagascar, Myanmar, Sri Lanka, and Thailand. Brazil is also a key producer of purple and pink sapphires.

FACETED

RUBY
Corundum

The best known and most highly valued of the corundum group, ruby is red. The color may range from pinkish-red to purplish-red and dark brownish-red depending on the amounts of the chemical elements iron, chromium and vanadium. Variations in the amount available as the gemstone is formed also lead to growth features such as lines or zones varying in color from dark almost opaque to lighter red or almost colorless. They are strongly pleochroic and the color is enhanced by fluorescence. The name is possibly derived from the Sanskrit word *kuruvinda*, or from the Latin word *rubeus* meaning "red." Rubies are said to have the power to bring the wearer friendship and romance, energy, courage, and peace. Ruby may show asterism (seen as star stones) when cut *en cabochon* (as a cabochon). It is the birthstone for July.

The Timur ruby and the Black Prince's Ruby, the large red gemstone set in the front of the Imperial State Crown of the British crown jewels are in fact spinel. Although both ruby and spinel are red, they belong to different crystal systems. Rubies form as hexagonal (six-sided) crystals that may be barrel-shaped with flat or pointed (tapering) ends. Depending on color and inclusions, the value of a good quality red spinel may be similar to or more than a ruby of similar size.

The color and quality of ruby varies with their occurrence. Mogok (Myanmar) rubies are prized for their color and fluorescence which appears to make the rubies glow. Rubies from Sri Lanka may be paler, those from Pakistan, Afghanistan, Vietnam and Cambodia have a strong red color and Thailand rubies may be darker red or a brownish-red. The color may be improved using heating and other treatments.

Occurrence Rubies occur in limestone and in gem gravels. Myanmar rubies are the most famous because of their color. Other localities include Afghanistan, Australia, Cambodia, India, Kenya, Madagascar, Pakistan, Russia, Tanzania, Thailand, the USA, and Vietnam.

CABOCHON   FACETED

H9

SAPPHIRE (BLUE)

Corundum

The color of blue sapphire is due to traces of iron and titanium. Color variations occur, and care has to be taken when setting gemstones so that the best color shows through the front of the gemstone. Synthetic corundum can be produced with the color change of natural sapphire. Water sapphire is a trade name for another gem-

stone called iolite (cordierite) and should not be confused with sapphire. Color can be enhanced by heat-treating, irradiation and other treatments. It is the birthstone for September.

Occurrence The most valued blue color has come from Kashmir. Other localities include Australia, Brazil, Cambodia, Colombia, India, Kenya, Malawi, Myanmar, Nigeria, Sri Lanka, Thailand, and the USA. Color-change sapphires are mainly from Africa and Sri Lanka.

FACETED

YELLOW SAPPHIRE
Corundum

Pink and yellow sapphires from Australia have been used in gemstones fashioned as floral displays in brooches and rings. With a hardness of 9 on Mohs' scale, these bright and hard-wearing gemstones make attractive pieces. As with other sapphires, yellow sapphire used to have the prefix "oriental" and was called oriental topaz. Yellow sapphires have also been known as king topaz and Indian topaz. However, as topaz is a different gemstone, and in order to avoid further confusion, these names should no longer be used.

Occurrence Localities include Australia, Sri Lanka, Tanzania, Thailand, and the USA.

FACETED

DIAMOND

Diamond

Diamond is the most famous of all gemstones. With a hardness of 10 on Mohs' scale, it is also the hardest material. Diamond can only be scratched by another diamond and therefore, only diamond can be used to cut and polish a diamond. A lapidary, when deciding how best to fashion a diamond, will use the knowledge that hardness is a directional property, and that each diamond will have a greater hardness in one direction than another, when using diamond crystals or fragments to saw or polish a gemstone. The lapidary will also use cleavage, another directional property, in order to find the directions in which a diamond will break (cleave) along planes related to the atomic structure.

Diamond is sorted by color, cut, clarity, and carat (the unit of weight used in gemology)—the 4 Cs (*see pp 14–19*). The value of each diamond is assessed using the results of the 4 Cs. Diamond is formed of pure carbon. Its strength is due to the way that the carbon atoms are bonded in a strong 3-D structure. Most diamonds are formed deep within the Earth's crust at depths of 50–90 miles (80–150 km) and are brought to the surface as a result of volcanic explosions. Diamonds are mined from the vents and pipes of extinct volcanoes or extracted from river gravels and sands to which they have been transported during weathering and erosion of the volcanic rock (kimberlite or lamproite). Diamond is the birthstone for April.

Occurrence Diamond localities include Africa (including Angola, Botswana, Ghana, Namibia, Sierra Leone, South Africa, and Zaire), Australia, Brazil, Canada, India, Indonesia, Russia, and the USA.

FACETED

FAMOUS DIAMONDS

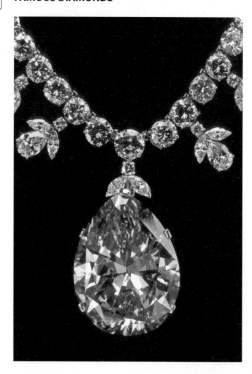

Diamonds with the longest history are those found more than 2,000 years ago in the alluvial gravels of India, in Borneo, and later from Brazil. It was not until 1866 that diamond was found in South Africa, and diamonds were first mined from the rock in which they had formed. The earliest Indian diamonds were not cut, as it was believed this would release the soul of the gemstone and reduce its powers. The largest diamond ever discovered is the Cullinan (3,106 carats), which was found at the Premier Diamond Mine near Pretoria (South Africa) in 1870. The Cullinan was cut as nine large brilliant cut diamonds and 96 smaller gemstones. The most famous of these is the Star of Africa diamond (530.20 carats) in the Sovereign's Royal Scepter of the British Crown Jewels. The Eureka's (10.73 carats) claim to fame is that it was the first officially recorded diamond on the African continent; it was found in 1866. The discovery of the Star of South Africa (83.50 carats) in 1869 led to the South African diamond rush. The diamond in the photograph on the left is the famous Victoria-Transvaal Diamond, found in the Premier Mine in Transvaal, South Africa, in 1951. The De Beers Millennium Star (203.04 carats) is probably the most famous of recent finds, due to the amount of publicity it received as a result of the failed attempt to steal it from the Millennium Dome in London in 2000. Other famous diamonds include the Taylor-Burton Diamond (see page 10), the Hope Diamond (see pages 10-11), and the Koh-i-Noor Diamond (see pages 22-23).

Left: Victoria-Transvaal Diamond necklace

FANCY DIAMONDS

Hirsh diamond ring

Not all diamonds are colorless. Many famous diamonds are known not only for their size and the legends or curses with which they are associated, but also for their color. The color is due to the presence of trace elements, such as nitrogen or boron, within their structure. Diamond colors include yellow, blue, green, brown, pink, red, gray, and black. Originally a marketing tool for Australian diamonds, brown diamonds are usually sold with names that describe their color—such as cognac, sherry, and champagne. The most famous fancy diamond is probably the blue Hope (45.52 carats), which is on display at the Smithsonian Institution. It is an Indian diamond, believed by many to be a cursed stone that has brought bad luck to its owners. The National Gem Collection of the Smithsonian Institution is noted for its fancy colored diamonds. Among them are the Blue Heart Diamond (30.62 carats), along with a cognac-colored diamond (36.73 carats), champagne-colored Victoria-Transvaal Diamond (67.89 carats, see pp68–69), yellow Canary Diamond (12.0 carats), intense yellow Shepard Diamond (18.30 carats), intense pink diamond (2.86 carats) from Tanzania, green diamonds from South Africa, and one of the largest deep red diamonds (5.03 carats) which, when purchased, was sold as a garnet. Other famous, fancy colored diamonds include the Allnatt (101.29 carats); green Dresden (45 carats) and Ocean Dream (5.51 carats); black Orlov diamond pendant (67 carats); Steinmetz pink, Moussaieff red (5.11 carats); and blue Heart of Eternity (27.64 carats).

FELDSPAR
Feldspar

Feldspar is the name given to a group of minerals that occur in rocks worldwide. Found in most igneous rocks and many metamorphic rocks, weathered feldspar is also in sedimentary rocks, sediments, and soil. Feldspars are aluminum silicates. They have varying amounts of potassium, sodium, and calcium, by which they are classified. Feldspar breaks along planes of weakness related to the way the atoms are arranged within the mineral (cleavage planes). There are two good directions of cleavage; one is perfect, breaking to leave a perfectly flat, shining surface. Light reflecting and refracting at the surface, and diffracting from layers (lamellae) beneath the surface of different compositions, or twinning, gives the characteristic array of colors (sheen or schiller) seen at the surface in moonstone and labradorite.

Occurrence Feldspar occurs worldwide.

Feldspar Series (Group)	Chemical Formula	Crystal System	Feldspar Species
Orthoclase feldspar	$KAlSi_3O_8$	Monoclinic	Colorless orthoclase (adularia)
			Yellow orthoclase
			Orthoclase (Moonstone)
		Triclinic	Microline (amazonite)
Plagioclase feldspar	$(Na,Ca)(Al,Si)_4O_8$	Triclinic	Labradorite
			Oligoclase (Sunstone)
	Sodium end member		Albite
	Calcium end member		Anorthite

ORTHOCLASE FELDSPAR
Feldspar

Taken from the Greek *orthos* meaning "straight" and *kalo* meaning "break" or "cleave," orthoclase is named because it breaks along cleavage planes to give perfect, flat surfaces.

Occurrence Orthoclase feldspar occurs worldwide.

COLORLESS ORTHOCLASE/ ADULARIA

Orthoclase feldspar

H6

Though most orthoclase is colored by impurities, pure orthoclase is colorless. Adularia refers to the clear or transparent orthoclase with a bluish-white schiller from Adular-Bergstock in the Adula Mountains of southern Switzerland. The schiller of adularia may be referred to as adularescence, though not all adularia shows schiller. Adularia is not the same as moonstone, but the two can be confused; although both may have a similar bluish-white schiller, moonstone is generally translucent, rather than clear or transparent.

Occurrence Colorless, clear orthoclase occurs in Madagascar. The best-known locality for adularia is Adular-Bergstock in Switzerland.

FACETED

YELLOW ORTHOCLASE
Orthoclase feldspar

The yellow color is caused by impurities of iron in the mineral. Yellow orthoclase is fragile and can break easily. With a hardness of 6 on Mohs' scale, it is not particularly hard-wearing. It is therefore usually only cut for gem collectors, and, when set in jewelry, a step cut or emerald cut (step cut with the corners taken off) is usually preferred. It may be cut *en cabochon* (as a cabochon), though this is seldom the case.

H6

Occurrence The best yellow orthoclase is found in Madagascar. Other localities include Australia, Germany, India, Mexico, Myanmar, Sri Lanka, and the USA.

CABOCHON   FACETED

MOONSTONE
Orthoclase feldspar

Moonstone is the most valuable of the orthoclase feldspars. Considered a sacred stone in India, moonstone is revered by many nationalities as a spiritual stone or dream

stone, associated with healing and protection. Its moon-like appearance and characteristic blue-white schiller are a result of light reflecting off layers within the stone. The layers are alternating layers of orthoclase feldspar and albite, an end member of the plagioclase feldspars or albite with orthoclase intergrowths. Thinner and thicker layers of albite and ortho-clase affect the color and the schiller. Moonstone is usually cut *en cabochon*, fashioned as a cameo or carved in the shape of a moon to show its schiller to best effect.

Occurrence The best moonstone is from Myanmar and Sri Lanka. Sri Lanka is the main producer, with moonstone found both in situ and in gravels. Other localities include Brazil, India, Madagascar, Mexico, Norway, Switzerland, Tanzania, and the USA.

CABOCHON   CAMEO/CARVED

MICROLINE (AMAZONITE)
Orthoclase feldspar

H6

Amazonite is the name given to the blue-green gemstone variety of microcline. The characteristic color is caused by lead and water. There may also be white, cream, or yellow veins or layers of plagioclase feldspar. Translucent to opaque, amazonite is usually cut *en cabochon* or fashioned as small carvings. Named after the Amazon River, legend has it that native Amazonian Indians gave green stones as gifts. However, these were probably jadeite rather than amazonite. Jadeite is not known to come from the Amazon; it most likely came from Guatemala.

Occurrence India is the most important source of amazonite. Other localities include Australia, Canada, Madagascar, Mozambique, Namibia, Russia, Tanzania, and the USA.

CABOCHON

CAMEO/CARVED

POLISHED

PLAGIOCLASE FELDSPAR
Plagioclase feldspar

H6

The plagioclase series comprises feldspars that range in chemical composition from the pure sodium aluminum silicate end member (albite) to the pure calcium aluminum silicate end member (anorthite). Oligoclase is at the sodium-rich end of the plagioclase series. Plagioclase feldspars form crystals in igneous rocks and metamorphic rocks.

Occurrence Plagioclase feldspar occurs worldwide.

LABRADORITE
Plagioclase feldspar

Labradorite has the most colorful iridescence of all the feldspars. The sheen or schiller, also known as labradorescence, is due to the reflection of light off calcium and sodium-rich layers, called lamellae, within the gemstone. The flashes of color shown by labradorite are often blue, gray, and violet, but they may be any color of the rainbow. When the full spectrum of rainbow colors is shown as the gemstone is moved, gemologists may call this rainbow labradorite. Labradorite is named after Labrador in New-foundland (Canada), where it was found by geologists in the 1770s. Labradorite from Finland is usually referred to as spectrolite.

Occurrence Finland, Labrador (Canada), and Norway are the best-known localities of labradorite and spectrolite. Other localities include Australia, Madagascar, Mexico, Russia, and the USA.

CABOCHON

CAMEO/CARVED

POLISHED

H6

OLIGOCLASE (SUNSTONE)
Plagioclase feldspar

Sunstone emits flashes of color like the golden rays of the sun. Sunstone is usually opaque or translucent. Transparent sunstone is rare and when found may be faceted rather than cut *en cabochon*, the usual cut for sunstone. In most sunstone, the flashes of color are due to the reflection of light off flat, platy inclusions of hematite and goethite (metallic minerals). Sunstone from Oregon, known since the 1990s, has copper inclusions. Care should be taken not to confuse sunstone with goldstone, the name given to an imitation made of glass with copper inclusions.

Occurrence The best sunstone is from Norway. Other localities include Canada, India, Russia, and the USA.

CABOCHON

FLUORITE
Fluorite

H4

The wide range of colors—including pink, yellow, colorless, green, and purple—makes fluorite an attractive gemstone. However, with a hardness of only 4 on Mohs' scale and perfect cleavage, it is fragile and easily scratched. Polished beads, tumbled pieces, and crystal fragments are used in jewelry. Although fluorite is found worldwide, the best known is Blue John, which is recognized by its distinctive purple or violet and creamy-white or yellow banding. Famous since Roman times, Blue John has been used to make large vases and ornaments. The name is thought to be from the French *bleu jaune*, meaning "blue yellow," after the colors of the banding. Blue John is mined in the North of England in the Peak District National Park. Although the famous Treak Cliff Cavern and Blue John Cavern are all but mined out, small pieces are still collected in the area.

Occurrence Fluorite is found worldwide. Localities include Africa, Australia, Canada, England, France, Switzerland, and the USA.

FACETED   POLISHED

GARNET
Garnet group

Not all garnets are red. They may also be green, yellow, orange, golden, brown, or black. Garnets are grouped together because they are silicates (containing the elements silicon and oxygen) and have a similar crystal structure. They vary in their chemical make-up, forming series of garnets, from one end member to another—for example, almandine garnet (iron aluminum silicate), pyrope garnet (magnesium aluminum silicate), and spessartine (manganese aluminum silicate) are end members of the iron-magnesium series, sometimes called the pyralspite series. Other garnets form the ugrandite series. Most garnets are not pure end members, but a mixture—for example, rhodolite is a mixture of pyrope and almandine. Named after the small red seeds of the pomegranate (from *granatus*, the Latin word for "seed"), garnet is the birthstone for January, and the zodiac gemstone for Aquarius.

Occurrence Garnets are found worldwide.

Garnet series	Garnet end members	Garnets	Mixtures
"Pyralspite" (Pyr-al-sp-ite)	Pyrope $Mg_3Al_2Si_3O_{12}$	Pyrope	Rhodolite (pyrope and almandine) Malaia (pyrope and spessartine) Color-change garnets (almandine, pyrope, and spessartine)
	Almandine $Fe_3Al_2Si_3O_{12}$	Almandine	
	Spessartine $Mn_3Al_2Si_3O_{12}$	Spessartine (Mandarin)	
"Ugrandite" (U-gr-and-ite)	Uvarovite $Ca_3Cr_3Si_3O_{12}$	Uvarovite	Mali (andradite and grossular)
	Grossular $Ca_3Al_2Si_3O_{12}$	Hessonite (Cinnamon stone) Green grossular Rosolite Transvaal jade Tsavorite	
	Andradite $Ca_3Fe_2Si_3O_{12}$	Demantoid Melanite Topazolite	

ALMANDINE
Garnet

H7½

Almandine garnet, with a hardness of 7½ on the Mohs' scale, is one of the hardest garnets and also one of the darkest of the red garnets (along with pyrope). Colored by iron, almandine may be transparent or opaque. It is found in metamorphic rocks such as schist and gneiss. Named by the Roman scholar Pliny the Elder (23–79 A.D.) as "Albandicus," possibly after Alabanda in Turkey, almandine is said to warm the heart and cure melancholy. Slices of almandine have been used in jewelry for thousands of years—for example, the Saxon treasures found in Sutton Hoo (Suffolk, UK) and in windows, including (it is said) a window or lantern on Noah's Ark, which may have been used to guide the Ark to safety.

Occurrence Localities include India, Norway, Pakistan, Russia, Sri Lanka, Sweden, and Zimbabwe.

CABOCHON

FACETED

ANDRADITE (MELANITE AND TOPAZOLITE)

Garnet

The calcium-iron andradite garnets include the yellow-green to bright green demantoid (*see p86*), the black melanite garnet, and the yellow-orange topazolite. Topazolite crystals are found in metamorphic rocks in mountains such as the Swiss and Italian Alps, but are seldom cut as gemstones. Melanite is found in metamorphic rocks and volcanic lavas and, again, seldom cut as gemstones. The type locality for andradite (the locality from which the gemstone was first discovered and described) is Drammen, in Buskerud, southern Norway. Andradite is named after B J d'Andrada, who described the gemstone in 1800.

H6½

Occurrence Localities for topazolite and melanite include Italy and Switzerland.

FACETED

ANDRADITE (DEMANTOID)
Garnet

Demantoid is the best known of the andradite garnets with its emerald green color due to chromium, and characteristic inclusions of byssolite fibers also called horsetail inclusions. Unlike most gemstones, the appearance of inclusions adds to the value of the gemstone rather than detracting from it. However, a clean stone is still more expensive than an included one. Demantoid is also one of the rarest and most sought-after gemstones. It has adamantine luster (luster of a diamond) and a higher dispersion than diamond, showing a rainbow-colored sparkle or "fire" masked only by the color of the gemstone. It is named after its resemblance to diamond, from the German and Dutch word *demant* meaning "diamond," because of its adamantine (diamond-like) luster.

Demantoid garnets from the Urals in Russia were popular with the Russian royal family and were used in the jewelry of Faberge and Tiffany. By the end of World War 1, the source was depleted and gemstones were so scarce that mines closed. Following the discovery of a new source in Namibia in the 1990s, demantoid garnet was once again available and the public interest in this bright emerald-green gemstone was renewed. With the increased interest, the Russian sources were re-examined and small-scale production was renewed and made possible. The Namibian demantoid garnet is of a similar color to the material from the Urals, but doesn't have the characteristic "horsetail" inclusions.

H6½

In order to make the most of its luster and color, gem quality demantoid is usually cut as round brilliants. Care should be taken when wearing, handling or storing demantoid as it can be easily scratched.

Occurrence The best demantoid is found in the Urals of Russia, where it was first discovered in 1868. Small-scale mining has continued since 1991. Other localities include Namibia, where it was discovered in the 1990s, Italy, and Tajikistan.

FACETED

GROSSULAR GARNET
Garnet

Grossular garnet has the widest range of colors of all the garnets, from colorless to pink (rosolite), orange, brown or golden (hessonite), and green (tsavorite colored by vanadium), and from transparent to opaque crystals. There are also massive specimens (those without a crystal shape) such as Transvaal jade, pink and green grossular (crystals and massive). Transvaal jade was first discovered in the Transvaal region of South Africa and resembles jade. A recent discovery is the Mali garnet, a light yellow andradite–grossular mixture found in 1994 in Mali.

Grossular is named after the yellow-green color of a gooseberry (botanical name *Ribes grossularia*). Pinkish grossular from Mexico is known as rosolite; it also occurs in South Africa and Madagascar.

Occurrence Grossular garnets are found in metamorphic rocks, alluvial deposits, gem gravels, and sands. Massive grossular garnet of a gooseberry color was first discovered in Russia, and is now also found in Hungary and Italy.

H7

FACETED   POLISHED

HESSONITE/CINNAMON STONE (GROSSULAR)

Garnet

The orange, brown, or golden color of hessonite is due to manganese and iron. Where the color is more like that of cinnamon, the garnet may be called cinnamon stone. Hessonite has characteristic inclusions giving the interior of the gemstone a swirling molasses-like appearance. Vedic astrologers believe that hessonite increases happiness and ensures a longer life.

Occurrence The best hessonite garnets are found in Sri Lanka. Other localities include Brazil, Canada, Germany, Russia, and the USA.

FACETED

TSAVORITE (GROSSULAR)
Garnet

H7

Tsavorite is the most sought-after grossular garnet with its bright emerald-green color caused by the presence of vanadium. First discovered in 1967 by the Scottish geologist Campbell R Bridges in northeast Tanzania, it was named by Henry Platt of Tiffany and Company, the famous jewelers, after the Tsavo National Park in southeast Kenya. Bridges also found gem-quality crystals there in 1971, just three years later.

Occurrence Most tsavorite is from East Africa (Kenya, Tanzania, and Zambia). In 1991, gem-quality tsavorite was also found in Madagascar.

FACETED

H7¼

PYROPE
Garnet

Named after the Greek *pyropos* meaning "fiery-eyed," pyrope garnets are mainly found in igneous rocks. They are popular in secular jewels of the 15th and 16th centuries and have been mined for more

than 5,000 years. Bohemian garnets, from near Bilin in Bohemia (in what is now the Czech Republic), were used in Bohemian jewelry, made with intricate patterns of many tightly-packed small pyrope garnets. This style of jewelry was particularly fashionable in the 18th and 19th centuries, and has regained popularity recently, although the garnets are now mined else-where. Pyrope garnets are often found as small rounded or water-worn fragments. Their blood-red color is due to iron and chromium.

Occurrence Historically, the Czech Republic has been the main locality. Nowadays, most gem-quality pyrope garnets are from the Yakut region of Siberia and from South Africa. South African pyrope is lighter than Bohemian, and has been called Cape ruby.

FACETED

RHODOLITE
Garnet

A mixture of two parts pyrope to one part almandine, rhodolite garnet is found in shades of pink and red and, occasionally, lavender. Typically found as transparent water-worn pebbles rather than crystals, their attractive colors and luster make them suitable as gemstones. They are named after the Greek *rhodo* and *lithos* meaning "rose stone" because of their color. A bright-pink raspberry color is the most sought-after. The name rhodolite was first used to describe pink-colored garnets found in North Carolina in the 19th century.

Occurrence Rhodolite with the best raspberry-pink color is mined in Sri Lanka, Tanzania, and Zimbabwe.

FACETED

H7

SPESSARTINE
Garnet

The manganese-rich end member of the pyralspite group. The orange-colored spessartine, named from the region of Spessart (Bavaria, Germany), has recently been found as gem quality in the Otavi region of northern Namibia. Bright orange spessartine garnets, also known as mandarin garnet because of its color, were discovered in 1991 in Namibia, with further deposits found in Nigeria in 1994 and, later, in Tanzania. Malaia garnets, discovered in the mid-1960s in Tanzania, have a composition with a range between pyrope and spessartine with some almandine, and range in color from orange to peach to reddish-orange. When all three ugrandite garnets (*see table on p83*) are present in a gem, it may result in a color-change garnet. Colors are said to be similar to those of the chrysoberyl variety alexandrite (*see p54*). However, true alexandrite shows red and green. Color-change garnet is more usually orange-red to brownish-red, purple or bluish-gray.

Occurrence China, Germany, India, Namibia, and Nigeria. Color-change garnets are known from Madagascar and Tanzania.

CABOCHON

FACETED

UVAROVITE
Garnet

H7½

The only garnet that is always green; the color is caused by its chromium content. It was named after Count Uvarov (1765–1855), who spent much of his life curating the gemstones of Russia, the country where uvarovite was discovered. Uvarovite generally occurs as crystals which are too small to be cut as gemstones.

Occurrence Italy, Finland, Russia, South Africa, Turkey, and the USA.

FACETED

H6½

HEMATITE
Hematite

Hematite has a silver-gray metallic appearance, though it may also appear black. Previously called haematite, it is named after the Greek word *haem*, meaning "blood." This is because ground or powdered hematite is blood red. The powdered mineral has been used as a red pigment in cave art since prehistoric times. It was used as a pigment in Egyptian tombs and Roman villas, and Native Americans continue to make use of the powder to mix their war paints, worn on the body and face during traditional dances and displays. Although heavy, because of its iron content, hematite may be cut and polished en *cabochon*, made into small carvings, or tumbled as polished pebbles mounted in jewelry.

Occurrence Hematite from northern England and Europe was popular for use in Victorian mourning jewelry in the UK in the early 20th century. Nowadays, most polished hematite is from Canada, Brazil, India, and the USA.

CABOCHON

CAMEO/CARVED

POLISHED

IOLITE/CORDIERITE
Iolite/Cordierite

Found mainly as water-worn crystals and pebbles in alluvial deposits, iolite (also known as cordierite) is strongly pleochroic. It shows different colors or hues (shades) of color when viewed from different directions. Colors seen may include an intense sapphire blue (another name for iolite is water sapphire), to a violet or insipid blue, to gray or colorless. Care must be taken by the lapidary when the gemstone is cut, so that the best color is seen through the front of the gemstone. It was named in 1812 after the French geologist, P L A Cordier. The name iolite is from the Greek *io*, meaning "violet flower." It is said that the Vikings used thin slices of iolite as a navigational tool because of its pleocroism.

H7

Occurrence Main localities are Brazil, India, Madagascar, Myanmar, and Sri Lanka. Other localities include Bolivia, Germany, Sweden, and the USA.

POLISHED   FACETED

JADE
Jade

Jade is the name given to two separate minerals: jadeite jade and nephrite jade. Both are tough rocks made of interlocking crystals and were thought to be the same material until 1863, when the two types were recognized. Although both are silicates, the mineral composition is different. Both are found as water-worn river boulders and pebbles. Jadeite is the rarer of the two, and is seldom found in the rocks in which it has formed (*in situ*). The color of nephrite ranges from dark green (iron rich) to creamy white (magnesium rich) material, while jadeite has a far greater range of colors, including the dark to pale violet and lavender jadeite. Jadeite may have a distinctive mottling or contain black specks, due to inclusions.

Occurrence The most important source of jadeite jade is Myanmar. Historically, Central America and Russia were also important. Nephrite jade occurs more widely.

JADEITE
Jade

H7

Jadeite jade occurs in a range of colors including green, white, red, orange, black, blue, yellow, violet, and the popular lavender. The best-known color is the emerald green jadeite from Myanmar. Colored by chromium and known as imperial jade, the translucent gemstone has been supplied to Chinese carvers since the 16th century. Jadeite has also been fashioned by the ancient civilizations of South and Central America.

Jadeite is usually found as river boulders. The boulders have a thick skin or "rind" hiding the gemstone within. Buyers purchase the boulders, without seeing the color of the gemstone, which is hidden within and surrounded by a thick, weathered surface or "skin" (occasionally a small "window" is cut into the boulder).

Occurrence The main source of imperial jade is Myanmar. Historically, Guatemala and Mexico were the main sources for South and Central American Indians. Other localities include Japan, Russia, and the USA.

 CAMEO/CARVED

 POLISHED

NEPHRITE
Jade

H6½

Green to cream in color, often with black patches, blotches, or bands, nephrite jade is exceptionally tough and hard-wearing. A venerated gemstone, referred to as the "stone of heaven" by the Chinese, nephrite carvings have been found in ancient burial sites, and nephrite has been excavated in China since about 5,000 B.C. Native North Americans from British Columbia (Canada) have carved nephrite for about 3,000 years, and nephrite carving by the Maori of New Zealand also has a long history. Tough as steel, nephrite is ideal for fashioning intricate carvings, and also for use as tools. In New Zealand, nephrite was used to make tools before metals were introduced by Europeans in the 18th century.

Occurrence Some of the best nephrite is mined in New Zealand. Other localities include Russia and Turkistan, Australia, Brazil, Canada, Mexico, Myanmar, and, of course, China.

CAMEO/CARVED   POLISHED

LAPIS LAZULI
Lapis lazuli

H5½

Lapis lazuli is a blue metamorphic rock made up of a number of minerals, including dark blue lazurite, golden specks of pyrite, and white veins or patches of calcite. The proportions of the different minerals give the rock its unique color and determine its value. Lapis lazuli has been mined from the Sar-e-Sang mines of Afghanistan for more than 6,000 years, and has been a popular gemstone with ancient Mesopotamian, Persian, Egyptian, Roman, and Greek civilizations. Still popular today, imitations include paste, stained chalcedony, and imitations with a similar chemical composition such as those manufactured by the Pierre Gilson laboratory. Powdered lapis lazuli was used to make the blue pigment, ultramarine, of Renaissance art.

Occurrence The best-quality lapis lazuli is from Afghanistan. Other localities include Argentina, Canada, Chile, Italy, Russia, and the USA.

CABOCHON

CAMEO/CARVED

POLISHED

Lazulite

H5½

LAZULITE
Lazulite

Lazulite is a rare mineral that ranges in color from a pale blue to an intense dark blue. It could be mistaken for lapis lazuli when polished, and pale blue lazulite may be mistaken for turquoise. Lazulite occurs as small crystals in igneous rocks that may be carved or polished as beads and small decorative pieces, or cut *en cabochon*. Lazulite is not the same as lazurite, the blue mineral in lapis lazuli, and care should be taken not to confuse these two names. Lazulite is named after the Arabic *azul*, meaning "heaven" (because of its blue color), and Greek *lithos*, meaning "stone."

Occurrence Localities include Austria, Brazil, Canada, Germany, India, Italy, Pakistan, Russia, Sweden, and the USA.

CABOCHON

POLISHED

MALACHITE
Malachite

The distinctive banding of malachite, from a very dark green, through dark to light green, is caused by a difference in crystal size; smaller crystals give a lighter color and larger crystals a darker color. Malachite is found worldwide and is generally associated with the major copper-mining areas such as those of Chile and Zaire. Malachite is often found with blue azurite, the blue and green forming an attractive gemstone called azurmalachite. Valued as a gemstone since ancient times, powdered malachite has also been used as a pigment. As an ornamental stone, malachite has been used as inlay in table tops, carved as vases, bowls, and statues. Large pieces have been used in buildings, carved as columns or cut as thin slabs to line walls. Banded malachite from Chessy (France) may be called chessylite.

Occurrence The most famous are the Russian deposits from the Urals. Other localities include Africa, Australia, Chile, China, Democratic Republic of Congo, France, Germany, and the USA.

CABOCHON   POLISHED

OPAL
Opal

H6

Opal is a hardened silica gel which can fill fissures and cracks in rocks, as well as replacing hard parts of animals and plants, or fossils including the shell, bones or teeth. It may also replace organic material such as wood (wood opal) or form stalactites and stalagmites. Opal usually contains about 5–10 percent water. Dehydration (drying out) may cause surface crazing

(showing a cracked pattern) or the gemstone may break apart. Precious opal shows characteristic flashes of color, called play of color or iridescence. Opal that does not show iridescence is called "potch." Romans considered opal as valuable as diamond. It has been imitated by man-made glasses such as paste and Slocum stone.

Occurrence Australia has been the main producer of opals since the 1870s. Other localities include Africa, Brazil, Czech Republic, Honduras, Mexico, Romania, and the USA.

BLACK PRECIOUS OPAL
Opal

The iridescence of precious opal is caused by the splitting of light into the colors of the rainbow (diffraction) by the regular pattern of spheres of silica which make up the opal. The colors shown depend partly on the size of the spheres, as their size determines which colors will dominate. The background color of the precious opal may be white or pale (white precious opal), colorless (water opal), dark, or, the most valuable, black precious opal, which is also the rarest of the precious opals. Precious opal is usually cut *en cabochon* for rings or as small polished pieces for brooches, earrings, and necklaces. Black opal is one of the birthstones for October.

Occurrence Lightning Ridge, New South Wales (Australia) is the best-known source of black precious opal. Other localities include Humboldt County, Nevada (USA) and Hungary.

CABOCHON   CAMEO/CARVED

FIRE OPAL
Opal

H6

Fire opal is a transparent to semitranslucent gemstone. It may show the play of color of precious opal. The best material is transparent and is usually faceted. Color may range from a pale yellowish-orange, to orange and dark cherry red. Fire opal may be the color of amber, but with a hardness of 6 on the Mohs' scale. It should not be confused with the softer organic material, as amber has a hardness of only about 2½ on Mohs' scale. Fire opal is one of the birthstones for October.

Occurrence The best fire opal is from the Hildago region of southern Mexico. Other localities include Honduras, Kazakhstan, and Romania.

CABOCHON   FACETED

OPALIZED FOSSIL
Opal

Organic material such as bone, tooth, or shell may be replaced by opal. Slices and tumbled pebbles of opalized wood may be used as decorative pieces in jewelry, and as inlay in table tops and other decorative pieces. Opalized shell may be mounted in a necklace, brooch, or pendant. Complete skeletons of fossils such as dinosaurs have been discovered replaced by opal.

H6

Occurrence Opalized shell and bone have been found in Australia. Opalized wood is famous from the fossil forests of the USA, including Yellowstone National Park (Wyoming), Colorado, Arizona, Washington, Oregon, and Georgia. Wood opal is also found in Sardinia, Italy.

CABOCHON   POLISHED

WHITE PRECIOUS OPAL
Opal

H6

As with black precious opal, white precious opal shows the play of color (iridescence) due to diffraction of light off the regular pattern of spheres of which it is made. The body color of the opal is pale, creamy white, or white. Opal has a hardness of 6 on Mohs' scale, and care should be taken both in wearing the stone and in storage so that it is not scratched by harder gemstones. Care should also be taken to avoid an opal drying out, which will lead to damage—including crazing (cracking) of the surface or the gemstone breaking.

Occurrence The most famous localities for white precious opal are Lightning Ridge (New South Wales, Australia) and the opal mines of Coober Pedy (South Australia), where opal miners live underground to avoid the heat of the day. Other localities include the Brazil, Czech Republic, and the USA.

CABOCHON CAMEO/CARVED

PERIDOT
Peridot

H6½

Peridot is the name given to gem-quality specimens of the mineral forsterite. It is always green, although the color may range from a yellowish-green to a dark olive green, as the color is caused by the iron that forms part of its chemical composition. Peridot may have an oily or greasy surface appearance (luster). It has a high bire-fringence, and doubling of the facets can be seen through larger specimens. Small specimens may contain bubbles or inclusions that appear doubled. Peridot may fill vesicular (tear shape) hollows and bubbles in volcanic lavas. It is the birthstone for August.

Occurrence Historically, some of the best specimens have come from St John's Island (off Egypt), from where it was mined for more than 3,500 years. Other localities include Australia, Brazil, China, Hawaii, Myanmar, Norway, Pakistan, South Africa, and the USA.

POLISHED   FACETED

QUARTZ
Quartz

Quartz is one of the most abundant minerals on Earth. It can be found worldwide in rocks and boulders as crystals, filling cracks or fissures in rocks, or in river and beach pebbles, sand, or gravel. The name is from the Greek *krustallos*, meaning "ice," because it was thought that colorless quartz was ice that had been turned into rock. Quartz is crystalline (made of crystals), but sometimes the crystals are so small they cannot be seen without the use of a microscope. If this is the case, the quartz is called microcrystalline or cryptocrystalline (from *crypto* meaning "hidden")—for example, chalcedony and agate. Transparent, crystalline quartz occurs in a wide range of colors (*see the table below*) and can be found as small delicate crystals as well as huge crystals as much as 22ft (7m) in circumference.

Occurrence Quartz occurs worldwide.

Color of Crystalline Quartz	Name
Colorless	Rock crystal
Cream or white	Milky quartz
Pink	Rose quartz
Purple, violet, or mauve	Amethyst
Yellow to brown	Citrine
Brown, brownish gray to black	Brown quartz, smoky quartz, Cairngorm (brown quartz and smoky quartz from the Cairngorm Mountains, Scotland) or Morion (dark brown to black opaque quartz)

Amethyst

H7

AMETHYST
Quartz

The purple, pink, violet, or mauve variety of crystalline quartz (amethyst) is often worn by bishops and other clergy, and has been said to guard against drunkenness. The name is from the Greek *amethustos*, meaning "sober." The birthstone of February, amethyst can be found as record-breaking crystals in geodes so large you could stand inside them. These huge pockets form as gas bubbles from cooling lava flows get "frozen" in. Later, silica-rich solutions fill voids and deposit crystals. Amethyst can be heat-treated to produce a color change to yellow, which is then called citrine. Gemstones that are both purple (amethyst) and yellow (citrine) are called ametrine.

Occurrence Africa, Brazil, India, and Sri Lanka are the main localities for gem-quality amethyst. The color of the amethyst and type of inclusions can be used to indicate possible country of origin.

FACETED   POLISHED

AVENTURINE QUARTZ
Quartz

H7

Aventurine quartz is mainly green with inclusions of a green mineral (fuchsite mica) which reflect the light. Inclusions of other minerals give the aventurine quartz a range of colors, including brown (pyrite inclusions), greenish brown (goethite inclusions), bluish green, bluish white, and orange (pyrite inclusions). Gemstones may be polished or tumbled, or carved as small pieces for rings, brooches, or necklaces. Copper inclusions in paste (man-made glass) have been used to imitate both aventurine quartz and aventurine feldspar. The copper inclusions in the simulant, which is called goldstone, may be seen using a magnifying glass or hand lens (×10 magnification) as bright triangles or hexagons.

Occurrence Aventurine quartz is found in Brazil, India, and Russia. Other localities include Japan, Tanzania, and the USA.

CABOCHON

CAMEO/CARVED

POLISHED

H7

BROWN QUARTZ
Quartz

Brown quartz includes gray-brown (smoky quartz), brown-colored quartz, and black quartz (morion). Smoky quartz and brown-colored quartz from the Cairngorm Mountains of Scotland may be called cairngorm. Colorless quartz (rock crystal) may be irradiated to give gray-brown or brown quartz. This suggests that brown quartz that has formed naturally may be colored as a result of the natural radiation of aluminum-containing rocks. The change in color caused by irradiation can be reversed using heat treatment to return the quartz to colorless quartz. Generally, irradiated brown quartz has a stronger and more consistent coloring than quartz that has not been irradiated. As a result of the irradiation, there may be white coloring at the base of the crystal where it is attached to the rock.

Occurrence Although brown quartz is found worldwide, nowadays much of the brown quartz sold is irradiated colorless quartz. The Cairngorm Mountains of Scotland are famous for their dark-colored quartz (cairngorm).

CAMEO/CARVED   FACETED

CAT'S-EYE QUARTZ (CHATOYANT QUARTZ)

Quartz

The cat's-eye effect seen in some quartz when cut *en cabochon* is also called chatoyancy after the French word *chat*, meaning "cat." The effect is due to fibrous inclusions in the gemstone, and the reflection of light off the oriented inclusions such as

H7

crocidolite (asbestos) and horn-blende. Cat's-eye quartz may also have inclusions of the mineral, hornblende. Cat's-eye quartz may be pale yellow, golden yellow, or brown. The color may be enhanced or changed using dyes and stains, heat treat-ments, or irradiation. The unnaturally bright blue, neon pink, and orange-colored cat's-eyes, popular in jewelry, and as loose polished gemstones, are often simulants that have been stained and dyed to imitate quartz cat's eyes.

Occurrence The main localities of cat's-eye quartz are Brazil, India, and Sri Lanka. Other localities include Australia and the USA.

CABOCHON   POLISHED

HAWK'S-EYE (CHATOYANT QUARTZ)

Quartz

The cat's-eye effect that can be seen in polished gemstones of hawk's-eye is due to the fibrous nature of the mineral crocidolite (blue asbestos) and the reflection of light off

inclusions within the gemstone. The arrangement of the fibers is not always straight: gentle curves, bends, or sharp zig-zags add to the attractiveness and interest, giving individual character to polished gemstones. The blue-gray color of the crocidolite is retained when crocidolite and quartz form as intergrowths. Hawk's-eye occurs as slabs in rock, and is often found with tiger's-eye (*see opposite*). Hawk's-eye may be a precursor to tiger's-eye, changing to tiger's-eye as further intergrowths are formed. Hawk's-eye can be treated with acid to change the color.

Occurrence The main locality for hawk's-eye is Africa. Other localities include Australia, Brazil, India, Myanmar, Sri Lanka, and the USA.

CABOCHON

POLISHED

TIGER'S-EYE (CHATOYANT QUARTZ)

Chatoyant quartz

The cat's-eye effect that can be seen in polished gemstones of tiger's-eye is due to the fibrous nature of the mineral crocidolite (blue asbestos) and the reflection of light off inclusions within the gemstone. In tiger's-eye, the croci-dolite fibers have been altered (mainly oxidized) to hydrous iron oxide, limonite, which gives it the golden-yellow and brown color. The fibrous nature gives the gemstone a striped appearance. As the gemstone moves, light causes light-colored stripes to appear darker and vice versa, adding to the interest of the gemstone. Heating can enhance the color, producing deep red and brownish-red tiger's-eye. Some hawk's-eye (*see opposite*) and tiger's-eye have been acid treated to produce what is marketed as gray tiger's-eye. Hydrochloric or oxalic acid has also been used to bleach tiger's-eye to a light yellow color.

H7

Occurrence Tiger's-eye is best known from Africa, where it often occurs with hawk's-eye. Other localities include Australia, Brazil, India, Myanmar, Sri Lanka, and the USA.

CABOCHON

POLISHED

H7

CITRINE
Quartz

The yellow or golden-yellow variety of crystalline quartz, citrine, has been called lemon quartz or cognac quartz, or even Brazilian topaz. Citrine may be sold using these names—but beware: if it is not clearly stated that the gemstone is a citrine, it may cause confusion or even mislead. It should be remembered that citrine and topaz are different minerals, with different physical and chemical properties and, therefore, different values, with topaz generally the more expensive of the two. Citrine is often found with amethyst, though amethyst is more common. Amethyst and smoky quartz can be heat-treated to give citrine, which may be why it is sometimes called burnt amethyst. Gemstones may be called ametrine when both amethyst and citrine can be seen in the same gemstone. Citrine is one of the birthstones for November.

Occurrence Most amethyst and citrine comes from Africa or Brazil. Other localities include France, Russia, and the USA.

CABOCHON

FACETED

MILKY QUARTZ
Quartz

Named after its cloudy white appearance, milky quartz is found in many igneous and metamorphic rocks. It is also found in sedimentary rocks, gravels, and sands. When cut *en cabochon* or carved, its greasy or silky luster may be confused with opal. The cloudy appearance is due to inclusions. The cloudiness and intensity of the milky white color depends on the inclusions of gas and liquid bubbles: the more inclusions, the more cloudy the milky quartz. Milky quartz can be seen within other crystalline quartz. The most obvious are the phantoms seen within colorless rock crystal. Phantoms form during an interruption in crystal growth. The result may be a layer of inclusions, which appear to cover the surface of the crystal as they are enclosed by the continuation of crystal growth. The layer appears as a ghostly outline of a smaller crystal frozen within.

H7

Occurrence Large crystals are found in Siberia. Other localities include Brazil, Germany, Madagascar, Namibia, the UK, and the USA.

CABOCHON

CAMEO/CARVED

FACETED

H7

ROCK CRYSTAL
Quartz

Rock crystal is the clear, colorless, crystalline quartz. Rock crystal may be faceted, cut *en cabochon* or fashioned as beads, slices, geometric shapes (such as pyramids, obelisks, spheres, etc.), or small carvings, etc. Clusters of six-sided crystals are marketed as decorative pieces, and individual crystals are popular for their aesthetic and healing properties. Occasional large, clear crystal balls have been polished as spheres, or crystal balls, used by fortune tellers and psychics. Thin slices of rock crystal have been used in watches and radios, as quartz vibrates at a constant rate once excited by, for example, a battery or electricity. Since 1950, when quartz was first made synthetically in the laboratory, it has been used in place of natural quartz in watches. It is also used in lenses and other precision instruments as well as having many more uses in industry.

Occurrence Rock crystal is found worldwide. The most important sources of rock crystal are in Brazil.

FACETED

CAMEO/CARVED

POLISHED

ROSE QUARTZ
Quartz

H7

Rose quartz is a favorite because of its color, from almost clear with a slight hint of pink, to pink and even red. Rose quartz is usually found as translucent to opaque masses without crystal shape (massive). Clear transparent crystals are rare. Transparent rose quartz that can be faceted is found in Brazil. The material is generally polished and carved as beads or decorative pieces such as figurines, or cut *en cabochon*. Rose quartz with inclusions of a fibrous mineral dumortierite may show a cat's-eye effect (chatoyancy) or a star (asterism) when cut *en cabochon*. Usually, these effects are shown when a light is shone on the surface (reflected light). However, in rose quartz the effect is best shown when light is shone through the stone (transmitted light). Dyes and stains have been used to intensify the color of a very pale rose quartz.

Occurrence Most rose quartz is from Brazil or Madagascar. Other localities include Afghanistan, Canada, Germany, India, Russia, and the USA.

CABOCHON

CAMEO/CARVED

FACETED

POLISHED

RUTILATED QUARTZ (SAGENITE)

Quartz

H7

Rutilated quartz is colorless quartz (rock crystal) with inclusions of long needle-like crystals of rutile. The rutile inclusions may be red, black, or brassy yellow, and have a metallic luster. The crystals may be so fine that they have the appearance of wisps of golden blonde hair, which explains why rutilated quartz is also known as Venus-hair stone. Another name is sagenite, but this should only be used to refer to rutilated quartz where the inclusions have been identified as rutile, and the crystals are not random, but are arranged in radiating interpenetrating, sometimes star-like patterns, with constant angles between crystals of 65°35' and 55°44'.

Occurrence Rutilated quartz is best known from Brazil. Other localities include India, Madagascar, Switzerland, and the USA.

POLISHED

TOURMALINATED QUARTZ
Quartz

H7

Tourmalinated quartz is colorless quartz (rock crystal) with
inclusions of long, often needle-
like, crystals of the mineral
tourmaline. Tourmaline crystals
have a distinctive triangular
cross-section; the triangle is
not a straight-sided triangle, but
a convex triangle with sides that bulge outwards. Tourmaline
crystals found within quartz are usually of the opaque black
variety called schorl, but may also be dark green (elbaite), dark
brown, or golden in color, and very rarely blue (indicolite). The
inclusions appear to be arranged haphazardly rather than being
aligned, which gives each crystal a unique appearance. Tourmalinated quartz is usually tumbled or polished as beads and
small irregular-shaped pieces, which are usually set in silver and
fashioned as pendants, necklaces, bracelets, rings, and brooches.

Occurrence Polished spheres made from Brazilian material
may be several inches across. Other localities include India,
Madagascar, Switzerland, and the USA.

POLISHED

RHODOCHROSITE
Rhodochrosite

Rhodochrosite is named after the Greek words *rhodon* meaning "rose" and *chroma* meaning "color," after the pink to red color caused by manganese. Rhodo-chrosite rarely occurs as transparent crystals large enough to facet. Although good-quality gemstones have been found in, for example, Colorado, and have been cut for collectors, they do not make good hard-wearing gemstones, as they are brittle and relatively soft (hardness 4 on Mohs' scale). More often, rhodochrosite occurs as banded rocks or stalac-tites, which, when cut and polished, show a concentric pattern of light and dark pink, red or white uneven circles. Rhodo-chrosite has also been known as Inca rose, named after the Incas who worked the silver mines of Argentina.

Occurrence Rhodochrosite has been mined in Argentina since the 13th century. The main producer is now the USA. Other localities include Brazil, Canada, Mexico, Peru, and South Africa.

CABOCHON

CAMEO/CARVED

POLISHED

RHODONITE
Rhodonite

H6

Rhodonite should not to be confused with rhodochrosite (similar color) or rhodolite garnet (similar spelling), whose names are derived from the Greek *rhodon/rhodos* meaning "rose," which refers to their similar rose color. Rhodonite very rarely occurs as crystals, and is usually found as opaque or translucent massive (without crystal shape) specimens with black veins or patches caused by manganese oxide. The presence of black patches should distinguish it from rhodochrosite at a glance. Where black patches are absent, further tests may be needed to distinguish the two minerals. Rhodonite is harder-wearing than rhodochrosite and more suitable as a gemstone. Massive material is usually cut *en cabochon*, polished as beads, used in cameos or made into small carvings. Large slabs can be used as facades (decorative panels) on walls.

Occurrence The main localities are Australia and Russia. Other localities include Brazil, Canada, Mexico, New Zealand, and the USA.

CABOCHON

CAMEO/CARVED

POLISHED

Spinel

H8

SPINEL
Spinel

Spinel occurs in a range of colors including pale violet, pink, blue, mauve, gray-blue, blue, and black, but the red spinel is the best known. Both red spinel (also known as balas ruby) and ruby are colored by chromium, and it is this similarity, as well as a similar hardness, luster, and density, that has led to confusion. The famous gemstone called the Black Prince's Ruby in the Imperial State Crown of the British Crown Jewels is, in fact, a spinel (there is a small ruby embedded in the spinel). Spinel is found in igneous rocks and in river gravels. Synthetic spinel has been manufactured in the laboratory since 1910, and has been used to imitate gemstones, including ruby and diamond.

Occurrence Main localities are India, Madagascar, Myanmar, and Sri Lanka.
Other localities include
Afghanistan, Australia, Brazil,
Pakistan, Russia, and the USA.

CABOCHON   FACETED

TAAFFEITE (MAGNESIOTAAFFEITE)

Taaffeite (magnesiotaaffeite)

Taaffeite is a very rare gemstone, which ranges in color from near-colorless to pink, red, mauve, brownish-purple, blue, greenish, and violet. The gemstone is famous for being the first to be identified as a new mineral having already been faceted as a gemstone.

H8

Taaffeite is named after Count C R Taaffe (1898–1967), who found the gemstone in a jeweler's shop in Dublin, Ireland, in 1945. It was initially thought to be a mauve spinel, but, on further testing, was found to be a new mineral. The results were published in *Mineralogical Magazine* in 1951 in a paper by several mineralogists and gemologists from the Natural History Museum and The Gemmological Association and Gem Testing Laboratory of Great Britain.

Occurrence Taaffeite has been found in gem gravels in Sri Lanka, and in Tanzania and China, but not in the rock in which it was formed.

FACETED

TOPAZ
Topaz

Topaz occurs in a range of colors including colorless, pink, brown, golden-yellow (sherry topaz), gray-green, green, and blue. It is found in igneous rocks, including pegmatites, granites, and volcanic lavas. Water-worn pebbles found in alluvial deposits may have a surface like frosted glass. Topaz has a hardness of 8 on the Mohs' scale, a greasy feel and adamantine luster. Care should be taken not to damage topaz crystals and cut gemstones, as they may break along one direction of perfect cleavage (leaving a completely flat surface). Colorless or pale brown topaz may be irradiated and heat-treated to give bright blue gemstones. Yellow topaz can be heat-treated to give the rarer pink topaz. Topaz is one of the birthstones for November.

Occurrence Brazil, Myanmar, Sri Lanka, and the USA. Pink topaz is found in Brazil, Pakistan, and Russia.

FACETED

A selection of topaz cut stones

TOURMALINE
Tourmaline

Tourmaline has a wider range of colors than any other gemstone. The addition of small amounts of trace elements such as iron, manganese, chromium, vanadium, titanium, and copper to the already complex chemical composition causes the different colors. The mineralogy of the tourmaline group is complex. Members of the tourmaline group with the same color may have a different chemical composition, but gemstones are usually named by their color rather than their mineralogy. Schorl, the black tourmaline, is the most common.

Most transparent-colored tourmaline used as gemstones is from the elbaite subgroup, named after the Italian island of Elba. Within a single crystal, tourmaline may show many colors (parti-colored). The color or intensity of color may also vary when viewed from different directions (pleochroism). The best color is usually seen when viewed along the long axis of a crystal (as if looking straight into the point of the crystal). Care must be taken by the lapidary, so that the best color is seen when the gemstone is viewed through the front of the stone. Pink tourmaline is one of the birthstones for October. To show the color to its best advantage, tourmaline may be cut at round brilliants, rectangular cuts or carved. Star stones are cut en cabochon (as cabochons).

Occurrence The main tourmaline localities are Africa (Kenya, Mozambique, Namibia, and Tanzania) and Brazil. Other localities include Afghanistan, Madagascar, Pakistan, Sri Lanka, and the USA.

H7½

Mineral species	Gem Name (varieties)	Common Gem Name	Color
Elbaite	Achroite	Achroite Colorless tourmaline	Colorless
	Verdelite	Green tourmaline	Green
	Rubellite	Rubellite Pink tourmaline	Pink to red
	Indicolite	Indicolite (indigolite) Blue tourmaline	Dark blue
		Paraiba tourmaline	Neon blue, turquoise, green
		Siberite	Violet-blue to reddish-blue
	Parti-colored tourmaline	Watermelon tourmaline	Pink core with a green rim
		Bi-colored (2), tri-colored (3), or parti-colored (more than 1) tourmaline	Various colors
			Yellow
Dravite		Dravite	Light brown to dark-brown, brownish-black and dark-yellow
Schorl	Schorl	Schorl	Black

Other tourmaline minerals include: Buergerite, named after Professor Martin J Buerger, a crystallographer; Liddicoatite, named after Richard T Liddicoat of the Gemological Institute of America; Uvite, named after the Uva district in Sri Lanka; and Chromdravite, an emerald-green colored tourmaline.

ACHROITE (ELBAITE)
Tourmaline

H7½

Achroite is the transparent to translucent colorless tourmaline, a variety of elbaite. It is named from the Greek word *achroos*, meaning "without color" or "colorless." As it is colorless, it does not show the pleochroism seen in colored tourmaline and can, therefore, be cut and set in jewelry in any direction. Fibrous achroite may be faceted or cut *en cabochon*. Pink tourmaline can be heat-treated to remove its color, giving the rarer achroite.

Occurrence The main locality is in southwest England. Other localities include Afghanistan, Madagascar, and the USA.

CABOCHON

FACETED

INDICOLITE/INDIGOLITE (ELBAITE)

Tourmaline

Dark blue tourmaline is called indicolite or indigolite by gemologists. Blue tourmaline is usually elbaite tourmaline. Where the color is considered too dark, it may be heat-treated to lighten the color.

H7½

Bright neon-blue tourmaline from Paraiba (Brazil) is called paraiba tourmaline (*see opposite*). Lilac to violet-blue tour-maline, first found in Russia, is called siberite (*see p136*). In Russia, indicolite tourmaline is found in granites and the clays formed from weathered granite. Crystals may be pencil-thin, striations (ribs or grooves in the surface) are obvious, and the cross-section shows a triangle with a curved outline (bulging outwards).

Occurrence Localities include Brazil (blue-green), Madagascar (blue), Pakistan, Russia, and the USA.

FACETED

PARAIBA (ELBAITE)

Tourmaline

H7½

Following years of exploration by Heitor Dimas Barbosa at the Batalha Mines in Brazil, paraiba tourmaline was found in 1989. Following the find, there was a rush to discover more, and an area of about 95,680sq yd (80,000sq m) was virtually leveled as a result of the number of tunnels dug by enthusiastic miners and gem collectors. The tourmaline is named after Paraiba, the state in Brazil where it was discovered. Paraiba tourmaline is sought-after because of its distinctive color and rarity. Sometimes described as neon blue, the vivid turquoise blue to blue-green is due to copper, sometimes with additional manganese.

Occurrence The Batalha Mines of Paraiba, Brazil, are the only locality for paraiba tourmaline. Tourmaline from Mozambique and Nigeria, which has a similar color, has been sold as paraiba tourmaline.

FACETED

H7½

SIBERITE (ELBAITE)
Tourmaline

Siberite is named after the violet to violet-blue colored tourmaline which was first found in Siberia, Russia. Crystals are usually opaque. Siberite is in the elbaite group and is a type of indicolite tourmaline. Siberite crystals have a curved triangular cross-section (bulging out) and vertical striations along the length of the crystal.

Occurrence Localities include Brazil, Namibia, Pakistan, and Russia.

FACETED

RUBELLITE (ELBAITE)

Tourmaline

H7½

Pink and red tourmaline is called rubellite after the Latin word for red. Rubellite is usually, though not always, elbaite tourmaline, which includes most of the colors of the rainbow. Rubellite was a favorite of the last Empress of China, Ts'u Hsi. She is said to have bought a ton of rubellite from the Himalaya Mine in California, and to have had a pillow made of rubellite. Crystals are striated and have a curved triangular cross-section which bulges out. The darker red rubellite is similar to the color of spinel or ruby, and is sought-after for its rarity. The bright pinks are popular for their color. Fibrous rubellite may be cut *en cabochon* to show the cat's-eye effect.

Occurrence Localities include Afghanistan, Brazil, Canada, East Africa (particularly Nigeria), Madagascar, Myanmar, Russia, and the USA.

CABOCHON   FACETED

GREEN TOURMALINE (ELBAITE)
Tourmaline

H7½

The color of this tourmaline varies from a dark brownish-green, through green, to bright emerald green. An emerald-green colored tourmaline, sometimes sold as chrome tourmaline, is colored by chrome. Chromdravite tourmaline may have a bright emerald-green color, and is in the chromdravite mineral group rather than elbaite tourmaline. Emerald-green tourmaline from Tanzania is sold as chrome tourmaline.

Occurrence Localities for green tourmaline include Brazil, Kenya, Madagascar, Namibia, Nigeria, Sweden, Tanzania, and the UK. Emerald-green colored tourmaline is found in Brazil, Namibia, Nigeria, and Tanzania.

CAMEO/CARVED

FACETED

YELLOW TOURMALINE (ELBAITE)
Tourmaline

A greenish-yellow or yellow colored elbaite tourmaline, the crystals may be transparent or translucent. Fibrous yellow tourmaline from, for example, Sri Lanka or China, may be faceted or cut *en cabochon*. Yellow tourmaline usually has a

H7½

brownish-yellow color. In 1990, a bright yellow tourmaline was discovered in Malawi, East Africa. The gemstones, colored by magnesium, have been described as electric yellow and have been sold as canary tourmaline, named after the bright yellow feathers of the canary bird. Heat treatment can remove traces of brown and enhance the color of yellow tour-maline. Golden yellow and greenish yellow tourmaline from Madagascar have been sold as yellow tourmaline (tsilaizite), and yellow tourmaline from Thailand has been sold as lemon tourmaline.

Occurrence Localities for yellow tourmaline include China, Madagascar, Thailand, Sri Lanka, and Malawi, the source of bright yellow "canary tourmaline."

FACETED

PARTI-COLORED TOURMALINE (ELBAITE)

Tourmaline

Tourmaline has a complex chemical composition, and small amounts of trace elements such as iron, manganese, chromium, vanadium, titanium, and copper affect the color. This complexity allows for a single crystal of tourmaline to show more than one color. These parti-colored tourmalines may show a color and colorless parts, or may have as many as twelve or so different colors. Parti-colored tourmalines may be faceted, polished, or carved to show two colors (bi-colored), three colors (tri-colored), or a range of colors. An orange and pink bi-colored tourmaline from Sri Lanka has been described as having padparadscha color. Care should be taken not to confuse this with the pinkish-orange corundum called padparadscha. Tri-colored tourmaline—for example, green, pink, and orange—is found in Brazil.

H7½

Occurrence Parti-colored tourmaline localities include Argentina, Brazil, Pakistan, Sri Lanka, and the USA.

CAMEO/CARVED

FACETED

WATERMELON TOURMALINE (ELBAITE)

Tourmaline

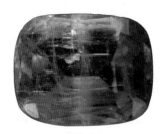

H7½

Watermelon tourmaline is bi-colored. The tourmaline is mainly of the elbaite and liddicoatite tourmaline groups. The crystals are color zoned and have a pink core surrounded by a green rim. When cut to show the cross-section, the colors are those of watermelon, with the pink fruit and green skin. Polished cross-sections are used in necklaces, brooches, and pendants. Watermelon tourmaline may also be polished as irregular pebbles, or carved as small figurines or animal carvings.

Occurrence Localities include Argentina, Brazil, Pakistan, Sri Lanka, and the USA.

CABOCHON

FACETED

DRAVITE
Tourmaline

This tourmaline is named after the Drave, the Latin for the River Drau in Slovenia. Dravite includes light to dark brown, to brownish-black and dark-yellow translucent to opaque crystals with the characteristic convex (bulging out) triangular cross-section. Crystals are heavily striated (ribbed) along their length. Double-ended (doubly terminated) crystals are hemimorphic, which means that the ends are different shapes. Dravite is the magnesium-rich tourmaline. Heat treatment can be used to lighten the color of dark brown dravite. Brown dravite tourmaline may be marketed with names that describe their color, such as light cognac tourmaline, golden cognac and sherry tourmaline.

Occurrence Gem-quality dravite is found in Brazil. Other localities include Africa, Australia, Canada, Russia, Sri Lanka, and the USA.

FACETED

SCHORL
Tourmaline

H7½

Schorl, the black tourmaline, is the most common of the group. Its color is due to the presence of iron. Crystals are opaque and have the distinctive triangular cross-section, where the triangle has convex sides (bulging out) rather than straight sides. There are strong striations along the length of the crystals. Crystals range from very fine needle-like crystals less

than an inch (a few millimeters) long, to record-breaking crystals many yards (meters) long. The name is from an Old German mining term. Tourmalinated quartz, colorless quartz (rock crystal—*see p123*) with inclusions of tourmaline, is fashioned as a gemstone.

Occurrence Schorl is found worldwide. Main localities include Australia, Brazil, Canada, Madagascar, Pakistan, and the USA.

FACETED

Turquoise

H6

TURQUOISE
Turquoise

The sky-blue turquoise of Iran (formerly Persia) has been mined for more than 3,000 years, and may have been mined in Egypt even earlier.

Also known as Persian blue, turquoise is named after Turkey, from where the Persian material was introduced to Europe. The color is due to the proportions of iron and copper; generally, the more copper, the brighter the blue and the less green. The surface is porous and may dry out, becoming dull or cracked. Polishing or impregnating the gemstone with oils, wax, or resin offers protection and enhances its color. Spiderweb turquoise has black veins of brown geothite or black manganese oxide. Since 1972, imitation Gilson turquoise has been used in the same way as natural turquoise—for example, cut and polished as beads or small spheres, or used in inlays and mosaics. Turquoise is one of the birthstones for December.

Occurrence Localities include Australia, Chile, Iran, Mexico, Russia, Turkistan, and the USA.

CABOCHON

CAMEO/CARVED

POLISHED

ZIRCON
Zircon

The adamantine (diamond-like) luster, hardness, and wide range of colors (including colorless, green, yellow, orange, brown, and blue) make zircon a popular gemstone. Zircon has been mined in Sri Lanka for use as a gemstone for more than 2,000 years. It is brittle, and care should be taken not to chip gemstones set in jewelry. Colorless zircon has been mistaken for diamond. Zircon should not be confused with cubic zirconia, an artificial stone that can be made in many colors to imitate a variety of gemstones. Natural blue zircon does occur, though much of the blue zircon that is sold is brown zircon from Thailand, Cambodia, Sri Lanka, and Vietnam that has been heat-treated to produce a range of blues, from pale to vivid neon. Zircon is one of the birthstones for December.

Occurrence Localities include Australia, Brazil, Cambodia, Myanmar, Nigeria, Russia, Sri Lanka, Tanzania, Thailand, the USA, and Vietnam.

FACETED

Zoisite

H6½

ZOISITE
Zoisite

Zoisite is named after Baron von Zois, who discovered the gemstone in the Austrian Alps. Transparent, gem-quality zoisite occurs in a range of colors, including yellow, green, brown, and the blue variety, called tanzanite (*see opposite*). An opaque pink massive variety, called thulite, is usually cut *en cabochon* or polished as a decorative gemstone. Thulite, from Norway, is colored by manganese. It usually occurs intergrown with white quartz, which may give an attractive pattern to the surface of the polished piece. Massive green zoisite, which contains ruby, can be polished as thin slabs, carved, polished as spheres, or tumbled as irregular shapes. Zoisite is strongly pleochroic. It may be heat-treated to enhance its color.

Occurrence Localities include Australia, Austria, Kenya, Norway, Pakistan, South Africa, Sweden, Tanzania, the USA, and Zimbabwe.

CABOCHON

CAMEO/CARVED

POLISHED

TANZANITE
Zoisite

Tanzanite is the blue zoisite. Named after Tanzania, where it was discovered in 1967, the trade name was introduced by the jewelers Tiffany & Co. It is usually heat-treated to enhance the color, as most tanzanite is a dull green or brown color when mined. Tanzanite is strongly pleochroic, and gemstones may show three different colors (trichroic)—red, purple, and blue—when viewed from different directions. The lapidary must take care to cut and set the gemstone so that its best color is shown when it is viewed through the front of the gemstone. In October 2002, the American Gem Trade Association (AGTA) announced that tanzanite had joined zircon and turquoise in the traditional list of birthstones for the month of December.

Occurrence Tanzanite is only found at Merelani, near the town of Arusha, ten miles south of the Kilimanjaro International Airport in northern Tanzania.

FACETED

ORGANIC GEMSTONES

The gemstones in this part are all organic. They are derived
from plants and animals. The organic material is from living
animals and plants—for example, pearl, shell, or bone, or from
the remains of dead plants or animals. Even fossils can be used
as gemstones; for example, amber is a fossil tree resin, and jet is
a fossil coal formed from the buried remains of ancient trees,
some of which are now extinct.

The gemstones here are mainly those that are polished or
carved rather than faceted for use in jewelry. They are generally
opaque or translucent (light can be seen through them, but
they are not completely transparent), and most are not as
hard-wearing as the mineral (inorganic) gemstones.

AMBER
Amber

Amber in jewelry is best known as golden or yellow polished or faceted beads that have a warm glow and may include insects, plants, or bubbles of air. Each piece may be clear or cloudy and will have its own character, color, and inclusions. Colors range from pale yellow to deep golden brown, green, and blue.

Amber is named depending on its occurrence (for example, simetite from the Mediterranean), or its appearance (for example, red amber, blue amber, green amber, yellow amber, black amber, and cognac amber). White amber, sometimes called bone amber or cloudy amber, has numerous inclusions or air bubbles that give the cloudy appearance. Heating in oil may clear cloudy amber. The most sought-after amber is clear and transparent, and has a bright yellow to golden color.

Amber is a fossilized tree resin. It floats in salt water, and irregularly shaped pieces of Baltic amber, released from on-land deposits or washed from under-sea layers, can be found as far away as Norway, Denmark, and the east coast of England.

Occurrence Amber from the Baltic region is the best known. Other localities include Canada, the Dominican Republic, France, Germany, Italy, Mexico, Myanmar, Romania, Sicily, Southeast Asia, Spain, and the USA.

CABOCHON

FACETED

POLISHED

Amber named after locality	Locality
Succinite	Baltic region, including Poland, Russia, Latvia, Lithuania, Estonia, and the Baltic Sea
Simetite	Sicily and the Mediterranean off Sicily
Burmite	Myanmar (formerly Burma)
Rumanite	Romania
Chiapas amber	Mayan mines in Chiapas, Mexico
Malaysian amber	Sarawak amber from Malaysia, specifically the island of Borneo

AMBROID
Amber

Although large pebbles
of amber have been
found, it generally
forms as thin layers or
nodules. Often, these
small pieces are not
large enough to be
polished or faceted as
beads for a necklace or bracelet,
or set in a ring, pendant, or earrings.

H2½

In order to make the most of these small pieces plus any scraps
left over as a result of fashioning larger pieces, they may be
heated and pressed together to make a larger piece. This is
called ambroid. The process may cause the flattening and
elongation of bubbles and inclusions, which may be used to
identify ambroid. Heat treatment may cause internal cracks.
Light reflecting off these results in a bright-colored reflection
or spangle, which gives it the name sun-spangled amber.

Amber is an organic material. Care should be taken not to wear
it in hot sunshine or very hot water, as it may lead to drying out
and cracking. Weathered amber may have a translucent, pitted
skin, and the color may mature to a darker golden-brown.

COPAL
Amber

Resin is a sticky substance, produced by some trees to protect against wood-boring insects, which acts as an antiseptic covering wounds in the bark. Copal is a modern resin and amber is a fossil resin. Although most resin can be clearly defined as either copal or amber, there are some "older" copals and "younger" ambers, where the distinction between the two is not so clear. Scientists continue to debate the use of the terms with the aim of defining the "cut off" between the two more clearly.

The color of amber is partly due to the source of the resin and the species of tree that produced it. Pale yellow to yellow amber is thought to be mainly associated with pine trees, and the darker, golden-brown amber is produced by deciduous trees.

Modern tree resins—for example, Kauri gum (copal) from New Zealand—have been used to imitate amber. Amber imitations may also be made of glass (paste), plastics and man-made resins (synthetic resins). Be aware: finding insects in a bead of so-called amber does not prove it is amber; they may have been added to imitations or modern tree resins to mislead.

Occurrence Localities include Africa (e.g. Kenya, Nigeria, and Tanzania), Australia, Indonesia, Japan, New Zealand (Kauri gum), and South America (e.g. Brazil and Colombia).

CORAL

Coral

Coral is a living rock; the structure is made up of both the skeletal remains of marine animals, called coral polyps, and living organisms related to the sea anemone. Corals may consist of individual organisms, which grow as conical or horn-shaped masses, or they may form part of a colony. As the polyps develop, they lay down a mineral skeleton which, on death, forms branch-like structures with a distinctive striped or wood-grain surface pattern, adding to the size of the coral. In this way, coral reefs can be built up over time. The most famous is the Great Barrier Reef, off Australia.

Coral

H3

Most corals are red, pink, or white, have skeletons made of calcium carbonate, and are generally associated with warm water. Black and golden coral are made of conchiolin—a tough, horn-like material. Red and pink coral have been harvested for thousands of years. The Romans gave coral to children to protect them from harm.

Following increased awareness of the importance of maintaining a healthy environment for coral growth, and as a result of the loss of vast areas of coral following pollution, changes in water temperature, and depth, coral harvesting has become more strictly regulated.

More than half of all the coral harvested is processed in Torre del Greco, Italy. Dull coral is polished to give a bright, vitreous luster and the wood-grain pattern incorporated in designs. Coral is usually cut *en cabochon*, though spherical beads and small slices for inlay work are also popular.

Occurrence Localities for red, white, and pink coral include the Mediterranean, and coasts of Africa, Egypt (Red Sea), Hawaii, Indonesia, Japan, and Malaysia. Black and golden coral localities include the coasts of the West Indies, Australia, and the Pacific Islands.

CABOCHON

CAMEO/CARVED

POLISHED

JET
Jet

The jet black of this organic material is as a result of its carbon content. Jet is formed from the remains of wood buried, compacted, and altered over time to give a hard, black, or dark brown coal that can be faceted or polished for use as a gemstone. The wood, which grew in Jurassic forests 180 million years ago, is related to the modern monkey puzzle tree.

Jet

H2½

Light in weight and with a hardness of only 2½ on Mohs' scale, jet takes a good polish and is easy to work with. Jet has been mined for more than 3,000 years. Worked pieces have been found in prehistoric burial sites and, during the Roman occupation of England, it was exported to Rome.

Following the death of Prince Albert in 1861, his wife, Queen Victoria, chose to wear black to show she was officially in mourning—a state she maintained for the rest of her life (another 40 years). Dark and somber jewelry was customary during periods of mourning, and jet soon became the standard gemstone of mourning. It has also been worn by the clergy, fashioned as rosary beads or crucifixes.

Occurrence Whitby, on the coast of Yorkshire (England), is the best-known locality for jet. Other localities include China, France, Germany, India, Poland, Portugal, Russia, Spain, Turkey, and the USA.

CAMEO/CARVED   POLISHED

PEARL
Pearl

Pearls form in shellfish
called mollusks (i.e.
oysters, mussels, clams,
scallops, and snails). The
mollusk is a soft-bodied
animal with a hard outer

shell. Natural pearls (*see pp160–161*) form within the mollusk
as a mechanism to reduce the irritation caused by the presence of grit, food, or some other irritant. They produce layers
of aragonite and conchiolin, the same materials that form the
shell, and cover the irritant with a pearl. These alternating layers
produce nacre, the mother-of-pearl that gives pearls their glossy,
iridescent surface.

For thousands of years, pearls have been collected by diving in
the oceans of the world (for example, from the pearl beds of the
Indian Ocean or the Pacific) or from freshwater rivers. The
depths at which marine pearls are found, and the fact that the
waters may be shark-infested, make their retrieval dangerous,
even with modern diving equipment. River pearls are easier to
harvest; they are generally baroque in shape (irregular).

There are about 100,000 species of mollusk, and each is capable
of forming a pearl, but without human intervention this rarely

happens. It has been estimated that only 1 in 10,000 pearl oysters will contain a pearl. The range of processes available, and the variety of species that are particularly suitable for pearl production for the jewelry trade, result in a vast array of pearls with different colors (including white, pink, purple, gold, and black), shapes (from perfect spheres to irregularly shaped baroque pearls), and sizes.

The shape and size depends on the species of the mollusk, the method (for example, the size of the nucleus), where in the mollusk the pearl formed, the length of time allowed for the production, water temperature and composition, and the health of the mollusk. Generally, the healthier the mollusk and the longer the time allowed, the larger the pearl. Spherical pearls are produced using a large, perfectly spherical nucleus.

Pearls are described depending on how and where they have been produced—naturally or cultured; in marine (saltwater) oceans or artificial ponds; in freshwater lakes, rivers, and streams or on land. Cultured pearls (*see pp162–166*) are categorized depending on whether they are nucleated (contain a nucleus) or not (non-nucleated).

Imitations include glass or plastic beads covered in a mixture of fish scales and varnish. Ammolite is a fossil ammonite (extinct shellfish) that has an iridescent shell of nacre. Pearl is the birthstone for June.

POLISHED

NATURAL PEARLS

Most natural pearls are marine pearls, formed in mollusks that live in the salt water of the oceans and seas. They have a smooth, lustrous surface. They are normally white or a silvery-gray, but may also be pink or black. The color of the pearl depends mainly on the type of mollusk, while the size depends on the mollusc and the length of time that the pearl has been forming before being harvested. These include the categories on the opposite page.

Marine pearls
Divers have harvested pearls from the pearl beds of the Persian Gulf, Red Sea, and Gulf of Mannar (off the coast of Sri Lanka) in the Indian Ocean for thousands of years. The Pacific Ocean, particularly around the Philippines, Polynesia, and Australia, also has a long record of pearl harvesting. Abalone (USA) and

conch shells (Caribbean, particularly the Bahamas) have been known to produce pearls, but they are very rare. Marine pearls, as with other pearls, are fairly soft and can be scratched easily. Spraying perfume near pearl jewelry should be avoided as the pearls may become discolored or etched.

River pearls

Pearl rushes, similar to the famous gold rushes of the 19th century, were sparked by discoveries of river pearls in the Mississippi River basin. Mississippi pearls were popular in the Art Nouveau jewelry of the 1920s, but river pearls are now very rarely found. In the 19th century, pearl fishing was also carried out in the rivers of northern Europe (including Scotland, France, Germany, and Austria), Scandinavia (including Norway and Sweden), and Russia. Scottish river pearls are still collected.

Seed pearls

Seed pearls are very small natural pearls with a diameter of less than $\frac{1}{10}$in (2mm).

CULTURED PEARLS

Cultured pearls have been produced commercially since the early 20th century. The vast majority of pearls on the market are cultured pearls from the pearl farms of Japan, China, Australia, and Polynesia (including the South Sea and Tahitian pearls). Cultured pearls may be dyed, bleached, polished (buffed), coated (for example with plastics), or irradiated to improve their appearance.

Cultured pearl production

Various techniques have been used to produce cultured pearls. The mollusk uses the same process as it would naturally (see p158), but in a cultured pearl the irritant is introduced artificially. A nucleated cultured pearl will also have a nucleus inserted.

1 A healthy pearl oyster is collected from open waters or from large enclosures where they have been bred (farmed) by pearl farmers.

2 The oyster is wedged open.

3 A piece of soft tissue (mantle) from another oyster and a glass or plastic bead (nucleus) is inserted in the soft tissue of the gonad (reproductive organ). The inserted mantle will become the pearl sack, which secretes the layers of mother-of-pearl (nacre) around the nucleus to form the pearl. Several beads may be inserted in a single oyster.

4 The wedge is removed, and the oyster is placed in a tray or basket and lowered into water suspended from a bamboo raft (in a pen, pool, pond, estuary, or lagoon, etc. near shore) where, for a couple of weeks, it recovers and begins to coat the nucleus with nacre.

5 Oysters that do not recover are removed. The remainder are transferred into trays and moved to larger pens or open

water further offshore, where they hang from racks at depths of 30–50ft (10–15m). They are left to grow for between six months and three years depending on the species of the mollusk, how fast the pearl is growing, and what size of pearl is needed. They may need regular feeding, cleaning, and health checks.

6 When the oysters are ready, they are harvested. The oyster is opened and the pearl removed. Soft tissue may be taken to be transplanted in another oyster to repeat the process. Removal of the pearl usually kills the oyster, but some of the larger species of mollusk may survive. Surviving oysters may be reused to produce more cultured pearls.

Mabe pearls are cultured by gluing a half-bead nucleus against the inside of the shell. Blister pearls grow attached to the inside of the shell instead of growing in the mantle; where they are joined to the shell, no nacre is developed.

Akoya pearls

Pearls more than ¼in (7mm) in diameter from the akoya oyster are generally from Japan, while smaller ones are more likely to be from China, Hong Kong, Korea, or Sri Lanka. They are fairly spherical and range in color from white, pink, and yellow to green, gray, and blue-gray.

Keshi pearls are tiny pearls that form as a larger cultured pearl is forming in an akoya oyster. They have not been cultured;

they just appear. They have the same colors as akoya pearls, but do not have a nucleus and form as natural pearls within the oyster. Keshi pearls are generally baroque in shape (irregular).

South Sea and Tahitian pearls

Cultured in the large mollusk, *Pinctada maxima*, South Sea pearls are the largest cultured pearls. They have similar colors to the akoya pearls; the white-rose and the gold-colored pearls are particularly popular.

Keshi pearls with a diameter of more than $\frac{1}{3}$ in (10mm) can appear during the culture of South Sea and Tahitian pearls. They are irregular in shape (baroque), have no nucleus, and may be termed natural. They are referred to as Tahitian or South Sea keshi pearls.

The only natural black pearls are those from the mollusk *Pinctada margaritifera*. Pearls may be dyed or soaked in silver nitrate to appear black.

Biwa pearls

The first freshwater cultivated pearls were produced in Japan's largest freshwater lake, Lake Biwa, near Kyoto, and sold commercially in the 1930s. Japanese biwa pearls occur as irregular pearls without a nucleus (the mollusk would not accept a nucleus). Production was interrupted by World War II. By the 1950s, freshwater pearls were sold in Japan as a less expensive and more colorful alternative to the marine material. Biwa became associated with freshwater pearls and, until recently, all freshwater pearls were sold as biwa, regardless of their origin.

Following pollution of the lake, Japanese biwa pearl production diminished, only to be replaced and surpassed in 1968 by freshwater biwa pearls from China, where production costs were low and technology and expertise was advancing. The early material was nicknamed "rice krispie" pearls because of their shape. Nowadays, biwa pearls from China are produced in a vast range of colors (including creamy-white to salmon-pink, salmon-orange, peach, wine-red, and violet, plus the more exotic peacock, copper, silver, and black-colored pearls), shapes (including rice, potato, stick, and square) and sizes. Chinese biwa pearls may have a nucleus.

Rice pearls

The shape of rice pearls (like wrinkled grains of rice) is due to the speed of cultivation, resulting in irregular thickness of the nacre and occasional pitting of the surface. Rice pearls are produced in fresh water—for example, in China. Other names used to sell irregular or fancy-shaped pearls include potato pearls, corn pearls, chiclets (square-shaped), lavender button pearls, plus copper, pink, or peacock biwa stick pearls—with stick-shaped pearls almost 3in long (about 7.6cm).

IVORY
Ivory

Teeth and tusks of animals such as elephant, walrus, narwhal, hippopotamus, sperm whale, orca (killer whale), warthog, wild boar, and the extinct mammoth are made of ivory. Tusks are large teeth that have evolved so that they stick out past the lips. The main component of ivory is dentine, which forms the main bulk of the tooth or tusk.

Originally the term ivory referred only to elephant tusks, but the chemical structure of teeth and tusks of mammals is the same, and the term is now used for any mammalian teeth or tusks that are large enough to be carved or engraved.

Mammoth tusk ivory carved more than 30,000 years ago has been found in caves in France. Ivory has been used to make piano keys, billiard balls, hair combs, chess pieces, inlay, small carved objects including netsukes (small Japanese sculptures), and jewelry.

Occurrence Historically, African elephant ivory has been the major producer of ivory; Indian elephant ivory is softer and yellows more easily. Other ivory producers include Europe, Indonesia, and Myanmar.

CAMEO/CARVED

POLISHED

IVORY AND TRADE

An estimated 700,000 elephants were slaughtered in the ten years prior to 1989, when a worldwide ban was introduced to protect populations of ivory-producing animals—particularly elephants. In 2002 the United Nations partially lifted the ban on ivory trade, allowing a few countries to export certain amounts of ivory.

Since then, bans and trading restrictions have been lifted or reintroduced intermittently as required, in order to protect elephant populations while also allowing legal trade. Trade in antique mammoth ivory is not illegal.

Modern ivory substitutes include vegetable ivory (part of the ivory nut palm), plastic, jasper, horn, and bone.

SHELL
Shell

Made of calcium carbonate, shells
show a wide range of sizes and
colors, from the iridescent colors
of pearl oyster shells (*Pinctada m
axima* and *Pinctada margaritifera*),
blue-green iridescence of abalone,
paua (the type of abalone that is
found in the waters around New
Zealand), and topshells (trochidae),
to the delicate white and pink layers
of the conch shell.

In addition to marine shells, a wide range of river and terrestrial
shells is also used as beads and in jewelry, particularly if they
show a colorful iridescence.

Occurrence Shells are found worldwide. Conch is found in
the Bahamas (where conch fritters are a favorite food),
Madagascar, and the Maldive Islands. Abalone mollusks are
found off the coasts of South Africa and the USA. Maori people
have a long tradition of gathering paua for its meat, as well as
using the shell in their carvings and as a *taonga* (the Maori
word for treasure). Paua has become the shell associated with
gifts from New Zealand.

Mother-of-pearl

Some shells have an iridescent coating of mother-of-pearl.
Mother-of-pearl is made of nacre, the same material that coats
a pearl. Nacre is usually a pale color, though the nacre lining
the shells of Tahiti can be dark. Where the layer is thick enough,
mother-of-pearl can be fashioned as beads, spheres or domed
cabochons, but thin layers are mostly used, for example, as low
cabochons, mosaic pieces for inlay, or as decorative pieces.

H2½

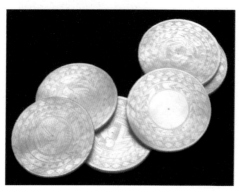

CAMEO/CARVED

POLISHED

Cameos

Shells that have layers of different colors may be fashioned as cameos. The outer layer is cut away to reveal an inner layer of a different color. Examples include the pink and white of the conch and the spider conch (*Lambis lambis*), the mottled cream and brown of the tiger cowrie (*Cipraea tigres*) with the violet inner layer, and the white outer layer of shells (including *Cassidae madagascarensii*), which have an inner layer of beige or brown.

Tortoiseshell

Tortoiseshell was made by warming and flattening the shell of the Hawksbill turtle and was used to produce, for example, tortoiseshell cases, hair combs and brooches. However, since 1973, this turtle has been designated an endangered species, and the sale of tortoiseshell has been banned.

GEMSTONE REFERENCE

The tables in this section provide a quick and easy reference guide giving further information about the gemstones listed in this book. They cover:

- gemstone name
- chemical formula
- crystal system
- hardness
- Specific Gravity (SG)
- Refractive Index (RI)
- Birefringence (DR)
- luster.

CRYSTAL SYSTEM

Gemstones are divided into crystal systems, which are a means of classifying them by their crystal shape and symmetry. There are seven crystal systems:

- cubic
- tetragonal
- hexagonal/trigonal
- orthorhombic
- monoclinic, and
- triclinic.

CUBIC

TETRAGONAL

HEXAGONAL/
TRIGONAL

ORTHORHOMBIC

MONOCLINIC

TRICLINIC

Axes of symmetry

HARDNESS

The hardness of a gemstone is given as a number on Mohs'
scale of hardness. The scale goes from 1 (talc), the softest, to
10 (diamond), the hardest-known natural material. The scale
is a comparative scale, based on 10 of the most common
minerals. Friedrich Mohs tested each by seeing whether it
would be scratched or scratch others in the group. By testing
each, he was able to put them in order of "scratchability."
A gemstone will scratch all those that are softer than it, and
will be scratched by those that are harder. Only diamond
cannot be scratched by any others, so is placed at number 10.

Gemstones that are assigned a mid value (for example,
emerald at 7½) do not have a hardness exactly halfway
between 7 and 8. They may be scratched by those with a value
of 8 (for example, topaz) or more, but scratch gemstones with a
value of 7 (for example, quartz) or less.

Mohs' scale of hardness	Gemstone
1	Talc
2	Gypsum
3	Calcite
4	Fluorite
5	Apatite
6	Feldspar
7	Quartz
8	Topaz
9	Corundum (ruby and sapphire)
10	Diamond

SPECIFIC GRAVITY (SG)

Specific gravity is a value of "heft," how heavy a gemstone feels. It is a ratio, a comparison of the weight of the gemstone with the weight of an equivalent volume of water. The higher the specific gravity, the heavier a gemstone will feel.

REFRACTIVE INDEX (RI)

As light travels from one medium to another it may slow down or speed up, causing the path of the rays of light to alter. As light enters a gemstone it slows down and is refracted (bent). The way that light is reflected at the surface of a gemstone, back towards your eye, or enters the gemstone and is refracted and then is reflected within before coming back out the front of the gemstone towards your eye, will depend on the refractive index of the gemstone and the way it is faceted.

Some gemstones, such as diamond, spinel, and garnet, are singly refractive: the light ray enters the gemstone and is refracted. Gemstones that have cubic crystals are singly refractive. In doubly refractive gemstones, the light entering the gemstone becomes split into two rays, each refracted (bent) to a different angle. Gemologists use an instrument called a refractometer to measure the refractive index (RI) of a gemstone, as a means of identification.

BIREFRINGENCE (DR)

Birefringence, also called *double refraction* (DR), is the difference in the refraction of the rays on entering a doubly refractive gemstone. It is measured using a refractometer, finding the largest and the smallest refractive indices, then working out the difference between the two to give the birefringence. When looking into a gemstone with a high birefringence, bubbles and cracks will appear doubled, as the rays of light have diverged sufficiently to have a noticeable effect.

LUSTER

Luster describes the surface appearance of the gemstone. Most gemstones have a glass-like vitreous luster. Other descriptions include the metallic luster of hematite, the greasy luster of turquoise and topaz, and the waxy luster of amber.

Name	Chemical formula	Crystal system	Hardness	Specific Gravity (SG)	Refractive index (RI)	Bire-fringence (DR)	Luster
Azurite	$Cu_3(OH)_2(CO_3)_2$	Monoclinic	3½	3.77	1.73–1.84	0.110	Vitreous
Beryl							
Aquamarine	$Be_3Al_2(SiO_3)_6$	Hexagonal	7½	2.69	1.57–1.58	0.006	Vitreous
Emerald	$Be_3Al_2(SiO_3)_6$	Hexagonal	7½	2.71	1.57–1.58	0.006	Vitreous
Goshenite	$Be_3Al_2(SiO_3)_6$	Hexagonal	7½	2.80	1.58–1.59	0.008	Vitreous
Heliodor	$Be_3Al_2(SiO_3)_6$	Hexagonal	7½	2.80	1.57–1.58	0.005	Vitreous
Morganite	$Be_3Al_2(SiO_3)_6$	Hexagonal	7½	2.80	1.58–1.59	0.008	Vitreous
Red beryl/bixbite	$Be_3Al_2(SiO_3)_6$	Hexagonal	7½	2.80	1.58–1.59	0.006	Vitreous
Chrysoberyl	$BeAl_2O_4$	Orthorhombic	8½	3.71	1.74–1.75	0.009	Vitreous
Alexandrite	$BeAl_2O_4$	Orthorhombic	8½	3.71	1.74–1.75	0.009	Vitreous
Cymophane	$BeAl_2O_4$	Orthorhombic	8½	3.71	1.74–1.75	0.009	Vitreous
Corundum							
Colorless sapphire	Al_2O_3	Trigonal	9	4.00	1.76–1.77	0.008	Vitreous
Padparadscha	Al_2O_3	Trigonal	9	4.00	1.76–1.77	0.008	Vitreous
Pink sapphire	Al_2O_3	Trigonal	9	4.00	1.76–1.77	0.008	Vitreous
Ruby	Al_2O_3	Trigonal	9	4.00	1.76–1.77	0.008	Vitreous
Sapphire (blue)	Al_2O_3	Trigonal	9	4.00	1.76–1.77	0.008	Vitreous
Yellow sapphire	Al_2O_3	Trigonal	9	4.00	1.76–1.77	0.008	Vitreous
Diamond	C	Cubic	10	3.52	2.42	None	Adamantine

Feldspar							
Orthoclase feldspar							
Colorless orthoclase	$KAlSi_3O_8$	Monoclinic	6	2.56	1.51–1.54	0.005	Vitreous
Yellow orthoclase	$KAlSi_3O_8$	Monoclinic	6	2.56	1.51–1.54	0.005	Vitreous
Moonstone	$KAlSi_3O_8$	Monoclinic	6	2.57	1.52–1.53	0.005	Vitreous
Microline/amazonite	$KAlSi_3O_8$	Triclinic	6	2.56	1.52–1.53	0.008	Vitreous
Plagioclase feldspar							
Labradorite	$(Na,Ca)(Al,Si)_4O_8$	Triclinic	6	2.70	1.56–1.57	0.010	Vitreous
Oligoclase/sunstone	$(Na,Ca)(Al,Si)_4O_8$	Triclinic	6	2.64	1.54–1.55	0.007	Vitreous
Fluorite	CaF_2	Cubic	4	3.18	1.43	None	Vitreous
Garnet group							
Almandine	$Fe_3Al_2(SiO_4)_3$	Cubic	7½	4.00	1.76–1.83	None	Vitreous
Andradite	$Ca_3Fe_2(SiO_4)_3$	Cubic	6½	3.85	1.85–1.89	None	Vitreous to adamantine
Demantoid	$Ca_3Fe_2(SiO_4)_3$	Cubic	6½	3.85	1.85–1.89	None	Vitreous to adamantine
Melanite	$Ca_3Fe_2(SiO_4)_3$	Cubic	6½	3.85	1.85–1.89	None	Vitreous to adamantine
Topazolite	$Ca_3Fe_2(SiO_4)_3$	Cubic	6½	3.85	1.85–1.89	None	Vitreous to adamantine

Name	Chemical formula	Crystal system	Hardness	Specific Gravity (SG)	Refractive index (RI)	Bire-fringence (DR)	Luster
Grossular	$Ca_3Al_2(SiO_4)_3$	Cubic	7	3.49	1.69–1.73	None	Vitreous
Green grossular	$Ca_3Al_2(SiO_4)_3$	Cubic	7	3.49	1.69–1.73	None	Vitreous
Hessonite/cinnamon stone	$Ca_3Al_2(SiO_4)_3$	Cubic	7	3.49	1.69–1.73	None	Vitreous
Rosolite	$Ca_3Al_2(SiO_4)_3$	Cubic	7	3.49	1.69–1.73	None	Vitreous
Transvaal jade	$Ca_3Al_2(SiO_4)_3$	Cubic	7	3.49	1.69–1.73	None	Vitreous
Tsavorite	$Ca_3Al_2(SiO_4)_3$	Cubic	7	3.49	1.69–1.73	None	Vitreous
Pyrope	$Mg_3Al_2(SiO_4)_3$	Cubic	7¼	3.80	1.72–1.76	None	Vitreous
Rhodolite	$Mg_3Al_2(SiO_4)_3$	Cubic	7½	3.80	1.72–1.76	None	Vitreous
Spessartine	$Mn_3Al_2(SiO_4)_3$	Cubic	7	4.16	1.79–1.81	None	Vitreous
Uvarovite	$Ca_3Cr_2(SiO_4)_3$	Cubic	7½	3.77	1.86–1.87	None	Vitreous
Hematite	$Fe2O3$	Trigonal	6½	5.20	2.94–3.22	0.280	Vitreous
Iolite (cordierite)	$Mg_2Al_4Si_5O_{18}$	Orthorhombic	7	2.63	1.53–1.55	0.010	Vitreous
Jade							
Jadeite jade	$Na(Al,Fe)Si_2O_6$	Monoclinic	7	3.33	1.66–1.68	0.012	Greasy to pearly
Nephrite jade	$Ca_2(Mg,Fe)_5$ $Si_8O_{22}(OH)_2$	Monoclinic	6½	2.96	1.61–1.63	0.027	Greasy to pearly

					1.50 (mean)		Vitreous to greasy
Lapis lazuli (lazurite)	$(Na,Ca)_8(Al,Si)_{12}$ $O_{24}(SO_4)Cl(OH)_2$	Various	5½	2.80		None	
Lazulite	$MgAl_2(PO_4)_2(OH)_2$	Monoclinic	5½	3.10	1.61–1.64	0.031	Vitreous
Malachite	$Cu_2(OH)_2CO_3$	Monoclinic	4	3.80	1.85 (mean)	0.025	Vitreous to silky
Microcrystalline quartz (chert and chalcedony)							
Agate	SiO_2	Trigonal	7	2.61	1.53–1.54	0.004	Vitreous
Banded agate	SiO_2	Trigonal	7	2.61	1.53–1.54	0.004	Vitreous
Stained/dyed agate	SiO_2	Trigonal	7	2.61	1.53–1.54	0.004	Vitreous
Moss agate	SiO_2	Trigonal	7	2.61	1.53–1.54	0.004	Vitreous
Fortification agate	SiO_2	Trigonal	7	2.61	1.53–1.54	0.004	Vitreous
Landscape agate	SiO_2	Trigonal	7	2.61	1.53–1.54	0.004	Vitreous
Fire agate	SiO_2	Trigonal	7	2.61	1.53–1.54	0.004	Vitreous
Iris/rainbow agate	SiO_2	Trigonal	7	2.61	1.53–1.54	0.004	Vitreous
Blue lace agate	SiO_2	Trigonal	7	2.61	1.53–1.54	0.004	Vitreous
Bull's-eye/ Cyclops agate	SiO_2	Trigonal	7	2.61	1.53–1.54	0.004	Vitreous
Onyx	SiO_2	Trigonal	7	2.61	1.53–1.54	0.004	Vitreous
Sard	SiO_2	Trigonal	7	2.61	1.53–1.54	0.004	Vitreous
Sardonyx	SiO_2	Trigonal	7	2.61	1.53–1.54	0.004	Vitreous
Chrysoprase/prase	SiO_2	Trigonal	7	2.61	1.53–1.53	0.004	Vitreous
Jasper	SiO_2	Trigonal	7	2.61	1.53–1.54	0.004	Vitreous

Name	Chemical formula	Crystal system	Hardness	Specific Gravity (SG)	Refractive index (RI)	Bire-fringence (DR)	Luster
Carnelian/cornelian	SiO_2	Trigonal	7	2.61	1.53–1.54	0.004	Vitreous
Bloodstone/ heliotrope/plasma	SiO_2	Trigonal	7	2.61	1.53–1.54	0.004	Vitreous
Opal							
Black precious opal	$SiO_2.H_2O$	Amorphous	6	2.10	1.37–1.47	None	Vitreous
Fire opal	$SiO_2.H_2O$	Amorphous	6	2.10	1.37–1.47	None	Vitreous
Opalised fossil	$SiO_2.H_2O$	Amorphous	6	2.10	1.37–1.47	None	Vitreous
White precious opal	$SiO_2.H_2O$	Amorphous	6	2.10	1.37–1.47	None	Vitreous
Peridot	$(Mg,Fe)_2SiO_4$	Orthorhombic	6½	3.34	1.64–1.69	0.036	Vitreous to greasy
Quartz							
Amethyst	SiO_2	Trigonal	7	2.65	1.54–1.55	0.009	Vitreous
Aventurine	SiO_2	Trigonal	7	2.65	1.54–1.55	0.009	Vitreous
Brown quartz	SiO_2	Trigonal	7	2.65	1.54–1.55	0.009	Vitreous
Cairngorm	SiO_2	Trigonal	7	2.65	1.54–1.55	0.009	Vitreous
Chatoyant quartz							
Cat's-eye quartz	SiO_2	Trigonal	7	2.65	1.54–1.55	0.009	Vitreous
Hawk's-eye	SiO_2	Trigonal	7	2.65	1.54–1.55	0.009	Vitreous
Tiger's-eye	SiO_2	Trigonal	7	2.65	1.54–1.55	0.009	Vitreous

Name	Formula	System	Hardness	Density	RI		Luster
Citrine	SiO_2	Trigonal	7	2.65	1.54–1.55	0.009	Vitreous
Milky quartz	SiO_2	Trigonal	7	2.65	1.54–1.55	0.009	Vitreous
Rock crystal	SiO_2	Trigonal	7	2.65	1.54–1.55	0.009	Vitreous
Rose quartz	SiO_2	Trigonal	7	2.65	1.54–1.55	0.009	Vitreous
Rutilated quartz/ sagenite	SiO_2	Trigonal	7	2.65	1.54–1.55	0.009	Vitreous
Smoky quartz	SiO_2	Trigonal	7	2.65	1.54–1.55	0.009	Vitreous
Tourmalinated quartz	SiO_2	Trigonal	7	2.65	1.54–1.55	0.009	Vitreous
Rhodochrosite	$MnCO_3$	Trigonal	4	3.60	1.60–1.80	0.220	Vitreous
Rhodonite	(Mn,Fe,Mg,Ca) SiO_3	Triclinic	6	3.60	1.71–1.73	0.014	Vitreous
Spinel	$MgAl_2O_4$	Cubic	8	3.60	1.71–1.73	None	Vitreous
Taaffeite	$BeMg_3Al_8O_{16}$	Hexagonal	8	3.61	1.72–1.77	0.004	Vitreous
Topaz	$Al_2(F,OH)_2SiO_4$	Orthorhombic	8	3.54	1.62–1.63	0.010	Vitreous
Tourmaline Group							
Elbaite							
Achroite	$Na(Li,Al)_3Al_6(BO_3)_3$ $Si_6O_{18}(OH)_4$	Trigonal	7½	3.06	1.62–1.64	0.018	Vitreous

Name	Chemical formula	Crystal system	Hardness	Specific Gravity (SG)	Refractive index (RI)	Birefringence (DR)	Luster
Indicolite/indigolite (including paraiba tourmaline and siberite)	$Na(Li,Al)_3Al_6(BO_3)_3$ $Si_6O_{18}(OH)_4$	Trigonal	7½	3.06	1.62–1.64	0.018	Vitreous
Rubellite	$Na(Li,Al)_3Al_6(BO_3)_3$ $Si_6O_{18}(OH)_4$	Trigonal	7½	3.06	1.62–1.64	0.018	Vitreous
Green tourmaline	$Na(Li,Al)_3Al_6(BO_3)_3$ $Si_6O_{18}(OH)_4$	Trigonal	7½	3.06	1.62–1.64	0.018	Vitreous
Yellow tourmaline	$Na(Li,Al)_3Al_6(BO_3)_3$ $Si_6O_{18}(OH)_4$	Trigonal	7½	3.06	1.62–1.64	0.018	Vitreous
Parti-colored tourmaline (including watermelon tourmaline)	$Na(Li,Al)_3Al_6(BO_3)_3$ $Si_6O_{18}(OH)_4$	Trigonal	7½	3.06	1.62–1.64	0.018	Vitreous
Dravite	$NaMg_3Al_6(BO_3)_3$ $Si_6O_{18}(OH)_4$	Trigonal	7½	3.06	1.62–1.64	0.018	Vitreous
Schorl	$NaFe_3Al_6(BO_3)_3$ $Si_6O_{18}(OH)_4$	Trigonal	7½	3.06	1.62–1.64	0.018	Vitreous
Turquoise	$CuAl_6(PO_4)_4(OH)_8 \cdot 5H_2O$	Triclinic	6	2.80	1.61–1.65	0.040	Vitreous to dull to waxy
Zircon	$ZrSiO_4$	Tetragonal	7½	4.69	1.93–1.98	0.059	Resinous to adamantine

Zoisite (including thulite)						
Tanzanite	$Ca_2(Al,OH)$ $Al_2(SiO_4)_3$	Orthorhombic	6½	3.35	1.69–1.70	0.010	Vitreous
ORGANICS						
Amber	Mainly $C_{10}H_{16}O$	Amorphous	2½	1.08	1.54–1.55	N/A	Resinous
Ambroid						
Succinite						
Simetite						
Burmite						
Copal						
Coral	$CaCO_3$, or $C_7H_{48}N_9O_{11}$	Trigonal	3	2.68	1.49–1.66	N/A	Dull to vitreous
Red coral						
Black coral						
Blue coral						
Jet	Lignite coal C and other organic material	Amorphous	2½	1.33	1.64–1.68	N/A	Dull to waxy

Name	Chemical formula	Crystal system	Hardness	Specific Gravity (SG)	Refractive index (RI)	Birefringence (DR)	Luster
Pearl	$CaCo_3.C_3H_{18}N_9$ $O_{11}.nH_2O$	Orthorhombic	3	2.71	1.53–1.68	N/A	Pearly
Natural freshwater pearl							
Natural saltwater pearl	$CaCo_3.C_3H_{18}N_9$ $O_{11}.nH_2O$	Orthorhombic	3	2.71	1.53–1.68	N/A	Pearly
Cultured non-nucleated pearl							
Cultured nucleated pearl							
Black pearl							
Irregular-shaped pearl							
Ivory	$Ca_3(PO_4)_2(OH)$ and organic material	Amorphous	2½	1.90	1.53–1.54	N/A	Dull to greasy
Elephant ivory							
Mammoth ivory							
Narwhal							
Walrus ivory							
Vegetable ivory							
Hippopotamus ivory							
Sperm whale ivory							
Bone (as ivory stimulant)							

Shell	$CaCO_3$ and $C_{25}H_{48}N_2O_{11}$	Various	2½	1.30	1.53–1.59	N/A	Dull to pearly to vitreous
Roman cameo							
Mother-of-pearl							
Conch							
Spider conch (*Lambis lambis*)							
Oyster (pearl oyster *Pinctada maxima*)							
Oyster (pearl oyster *Pinctada margaritifera*)							
Abalone (Paua)							
Topshell (Trochidae)							
Tortoiseshell (Hawksbill Turtle)							
Tiger Cowrie (*Cypraea tigres*)							

LIST OF SOURCES

BOOKS

Hall, Cally. *Gemstones*. 2nd ed. London: Dorling Kindersley, Eyewitness Handbook, Penguin, 2001.

Hall, Cally and Scarlett O'Hara, with additional material by Jen Green. *101 Facts about Planet Earth*. London: Dorling Kindersley, 2003.

Harlow, George E. *The Nature of Diamonds*. Cambridge: Cambridge University Press in association with the American Museum of Natural History, 1998.

Oldershaw, Cally. *Philip's Guide to Gems*. London: Philip's, 2003.

Oldershaw, Cally. *Rocks and Minerals: A Golden Photo Guide from St. Martin's Press*. New York: Elm Grove Books Ltd, 2002.

Oldershaw, Cally, Roger Harding and Christine Woodward. *Gemstones*. 2nd ed. London: Natural History Museum Publications, 2001.

Post, Jeffrey E, with photographs by Chip Clark. *The National Gem Collection*. New York: National Museum of Natural History, Smithsonian Institution in association with Harry N. Abrams, Inc., 1997.

Ward, Fred. *Jade*. Malibu, CA: Gem Book Publishers, 1996.

Ward, Fred. *Pearls*. Malibu, CA: Gem Book Publishers, 1998.

Ward, Fred. *Rubies and Sapphires*. Malibu, CA: Gem Book Publishers, 1995.

Webster, R. *Gemstones: Their Sources, Descriptions and Identification*. ed. with revisions Peter G. Read. 5th ed. Stoneham, MA: Butterworth-Heinemann, 1994.

O'Donoghue, Michael. *Synthetic, Imitation and Treated Gemstones*. Oxford: Butterworth-Heinemann, 1997.

Liddicoat, Richard E, ed. *The GIA Diamond Dictionary*. 3rd ed. Santa Monica, CA: Gemological Institute of America, 1993.

WEBSITES

Smithsonian Institution collection
www.minerals.si.edu/images/gallery/gem.htm

The Gemological Institute of America
www.gia.edu

The Gemmological Association and Gem Testing Laboratory of Great Britain (Gem-A)
www.gagtl.ac.uk

International Colored Gemstone Association
www.gemstone.org

American Gem Society
www.ags.org

American Federation of Mineralogical Societies
www.amfed.org

Mineral Data
www.mindat.org/index-A.html

INDEX

ACKNOWLEDGMENTS

'Dedicated to my wonderful daughters, both absolute gems'

Cally Oldershaw is a gemologist with an international reputation, an examiner for the Gemmological Association of Great Britain and former Curator of Gemstones at the Natural History Museum, London. She has written text books for gemologists and jewelers worldwide, as well as popular books on topics such as volcanoes, earthquakes, deserts, oceans, mountains, forests, rocks, crystals, minerals, geology, and landscapes.

PICTURE CREDITS

GEM HUT (http://www.gemhut.com) page 123; GEOSCIENCE FEATURES PICTURE LIBRARY pages 31, 40, 44, 58, 95, 122, 128, 136; HIRSH pages 60, 61, 62, 65, 70, 86, 90, 130, 135; ICA pages 27, 51, 55, 56, 85, 97, 115, 126, 137, 139, 145, 146; MAGGIE CAMPBELL PEDERSEN pages 149, 151, 154, 156, 158, 160, 162, 167, 169, 170; NATURAL HISTORY MUSEUM pages 23a, 23b, 28, 59, 66, 74, 78, 102, 113, 114, 116, 117, 119, 125, 127, 129, 133, 134, 138, 141, 142, 143, 152; THE SMITHSONIAN INSTITUTION pages 11, 12a, 12b, 20a, 20b, 29, 30, 32, 33, 34, 35, 39, 41, 42, 43, 45, 49, 53, 54a, 54b, 57, 64, 68, 75, 76, 77, 79, 80, 81, 88, 91, 92, 93, 94, 96, 98, 99, 100, 101, 103, 105, 106, 107, 108, 109, 110, 112, 118, 120, 121, 124, 140, 144, 147, 172; V & A MUSEUM pages 36, 38, 46, 47, 48, 50, 52, 72, 84, 104.

The Smithsonian would like to thank the following donors:
L. T. Chamberlain (page 39); Mrs. W. C. Crane (page 126); A. R. Cutter (page 118); Mr. and Mrs. H. Dibble (page 81); Evyan Perfumes, Inc. (page 29); B. O. Hawk (page 91); Mrs. O. B. James (page 105); Mrs. J. Logan (pages 12a, 64); Mrs. G. M. Morris (page 112); M. M. Post (page 30); R. Reeves II (page 20a); W. A. Roebling (page 107); Helene V. Rubin (page 32); Mr. and Mrs. M. Silverman (page 144); J. Sinkankas (pages 76, 80); M. Stuart (page 124); H. Taylor (page 45); Mr. & Mrs. L. Wilkinson (pages 68, 101); H. Winston, Inc. (page 11).

Edited by Sandra Stafford and Nancy Bailey for Cambridge Publishing Management Limited

Proofread by Jan McCann for Cambridge Publishing Management Limited